DESERT

Desert rose

Tuareg
cross

Lanner
falcon

Uzbeki
children's
mobile

Uzbeki camel drape

Tewa Indian
boy's rattle
decorated with
hummingbird
tracks

Jordanian
Bedouin
coffee
pots

Tadpole
shrimp

Tadpole
shrimp

EYEWITNESS GUIDES

DESERT

Tuareg
dagger

Written by
MIRANDA MACQUITTY

Photographed by
ALAN HILLS AND
FRANK GREENAWAY

Tuareg
dagger

Dromedary

DK

DORLING KINDERSLEY
London • New York • Stuttgart

Calabash for carrying water and food

Aboriginal knife

A DORLING KINDERSLEY BOOK

Project editor Caroline Beattie
Art editor Jill Plank
Managing editor Simon Adams
Managing art editor Julia Harris
Researcher Céline Carez
Picture research Cynthia Hole
Production Catherine Semark
Additional photography Andy Crawford
Editorial consultant Professor John Cloudsley-Thompson

This Eyewitness ® Guide has
been conceived by
Dorling Kindersley Limited
and
Editions Gallimard

First published in Great Britain in 1994 by
Dorling Kindersley Limited,
9 Henrietta Street,
London WC2E 8PS
Reprinted 1997

A CIP catalogue record for this book is available from
the British Library.

ISBN 0 7513 6023 6

Colour reproduction by Colourscan, Singapore
Printed in Singapore by Toppan

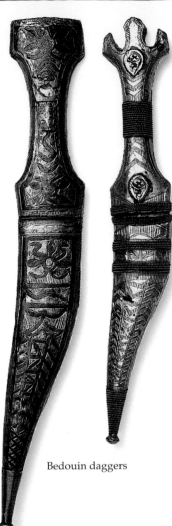

Bedouin daggers

Red spitting cobra

Bedouin man and woman from Jordan

Hopi Kachina doll

Zuni
shalako
necklace

Navajo
squash
blossom
necklace

Contents

What is a desert?

WITH LITTLE RAIN and extreme temperatures, deserts are some of the harshest places on Earth. A desert is strictly defined as a place with less than 25 cm (10 in) of rain a year. Hot deserts are found around the tropics, where the Earth's wind system brings cloudless days. This means that there are no clouds to shield the ground, which in the summer becomes baking hot during the day, but then cold at night as the heat is lost back to the atmosphere. Deserts at higher latitudes are cold deserts. Land formations also affect rainfall: some deserts occur within large land masses, such as Australia, where winds from the coast have lost all their moisture by the time they get there; others occur on the lee (far) side of mountains, where there is no rain left in the wind which has blown over the mountains.

NORTH AMERICA

Great Basin

Mojave

Sonoran

Chihuahuan

TROPIC OF CANCER

Atlantic Ocean

EQUATOR

SOUTH AMERICA

Pacific Ocean

Peruvian

Atacama

TROPIC OF CAPRICORN

Patagonian

FOG AND SNOW
Fog is common in coastal deserts, such as the Atacama in Chile, and the Namib of south-western Africa. Flowing along these coasts are cold-water currents; these cool down the air above them, and the moisture in the air condenses as fog. Fog is a vital life-giving source of water, but, in the Namib Desert (above left), it only rolls in from the sea about 60 days a year. While fog is common in deserts by the sea, snow can fall during the winter in cold deserts such as the deserts in the Great Basin Desert in the USA (above right). Frost can occur during the winter even in hot deserts.

PAST CLIMATES
Fossil remains of a small kind of hippopotamus have been found in the Arabian Desert, showing that 6 million years ago the climate was much wetter: hippopotamuses need lush and humid conditions. Remains from the Stone Age show that hippos also lurked in marshes once found in the Sahara, which has gone through several wet and dry climate cycles.

WEATHERED ROCKS *above*
Rocks in the desert are weathered or worn away by wind, extreme temperatures, and rare but torrential rains. Strong winds pick up sand, which then scours away at the rock, much like the sand blasting process used to clean dirt off old stone buildings. These sandstone cliffs are in the Jordanian desert. At the top of the cliff is a natural bridge (p. 10).

EUROPE

Mediterranean Sea

Kara Kum,
Kyzyl Kum

Takla Makan

Gobi

Negev Jordanian

Thar

ASIA

Sahara

Arabian

Sinai

INDIAN
SUB-
CONTINENT

Rub' al-Khali
(Empty Quarter)

AFRICA

Indian Ocean

Namib

Great Sandy

Gibson

Simpson

Kalahari

Great Victoria

AUSTRALIA

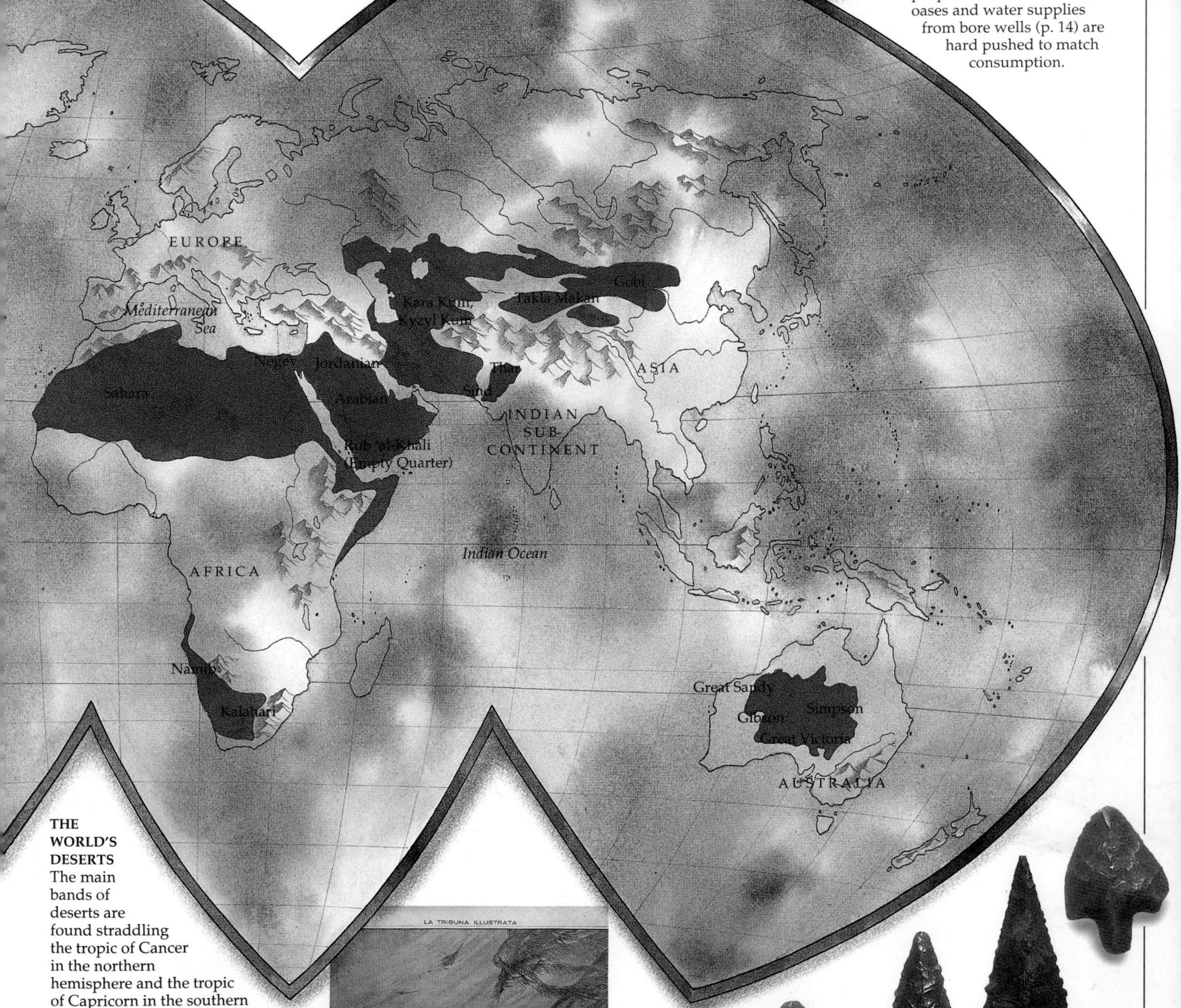

**THE
WORLD'S
DESERTS**
The main bands of deserts are found straddling the tropic of Cancer in the northern hemisphere and the tropic of Capricorn in the southern hemisphere. In the hottest deserts, air temperatures can reach over 50°C (122°F) and ground temperatures over 80°C (176°F).

LA TRIBUNA ILLUSTRATA

SAND STORMS
Strong winds are characteristic of deserts, as there are few plants to slow them down. The dry sands can easily be picked up to create a sand storm. The whirling sand can be so thick that the sky darkens, making it hard to see more than a few paces ahead.

Flint arrowhead, at least 4,000 years old

ANCIENT REMAINS
Deserts are good places to find archaeological remains because there are few plants to cover them up, and winds blow away the topsoil. These flint arrowheads from the Sahara were used to hunt birds and small mammals. They show that the Sahara was once a rich hunting ground.

What is a desert made of?

MOST PEOPLE THINK OF DESERTS as vast expanses of sand dunes, but deserts of rocks and stone are in fact far more common. Desert sand started out as rock, which over the ages was weathered (worn down) to form particles. The finer the particle, the further it can be blown by wind or carried by floodwater from the rare rains. Both wind and water sort the particles according to size. In some deserts, only the stones are left behind after wind has carried the sand away. Water dissolves minerals, such as salt, out of rocks, and these then recrystallize elsewhere. Desert soils are composed mostly of minerals from rocks; there is little plant or animal material such as dead leaves and dung, mostly because the weather is too dry for these to be broken down to enrich the soil. Some minerals, such as oil, are hidden deep within rocks below the desert surface.

DEVIL'S GOLF COURSE
This bed of rock-hard salt crystals lies in Death Valley, California, which is one of the hottest places in the world. Water draining from the surrounding mountains carries down dissolved salts, which then recrystallize and form a salt bed as the water evaporates.

WADI
After rare rains, water rushes along the wadi (dry river bed) in the desert in Jordan. The cliffs on either side of the wadi are sandstone, which is gradually worn away by the heat, wind, and rain.

Sandstone cliffs

Pink sand on the desert floor

Drought-resistant plants

BLACK DESERT
Black basalt, once spewed out as volcanic lava flows, now forms a vast stony desert.

DUST TO DUST
This soil from the Jordanian desert contains a range of particles, from dust to pebbles. When dust is picked up by whirlwinds, dust devils form: these are columns of dust that whirl along the desert floor. Once picked up by wind, desert dust may be carried far beyond the desert before it lands.

FINE SAND
This sample of red sand comes from Wadi Rum in Jordan, where it looks much lighter under the full glare of the sun. The sand is partly sorted into particles of a similar size by the wind. Bits of wind-blown plant material litter the surface.

COARSE SAND
Most of the sand particles in this sample from the Jordanian desert are of similar size. The sand comes from the bottom of a wadi, where any fine material is washed away when the wadi fills with rain water. Like most sand, it is made of the mineral quartz.

DESERT ROSE
Strange-shaped crystals like this one are formed within sand dunes in the Sahara. The crystal is made of the mineral gypsum. The gypsum dust, which is weathered from rocks, settles in sand dunes where it eventually dissolves in ground water seeping up from below or rainwater seeping down from above. Then the gypsum crystallizes into the characteristic petal shapes. Normally gypsum forms diamond- or arrow-shaped crystals, but the dunes' sand grains interrupt the crystal growth to create the desert rose.

The crystals form at angles to each other, giving the illusion of a flower

SAND-BLASTED STONE
A ventifact is a pyramid-shaped stone that has been worn smooth by wind-blown sand. It has three upper surfaces polished by the wind, and a bottom surface that is rough because it is not exposed to the wind. The three smooth surfaces are created by the changing wind direction. This stone comes from the Algerian Sahara. Bedouins travelling in the Arabian desert can tell which way is north on calm days by feeling stones, because they are worn and pitted on the side facing the prevailing wind from the north.

Gold nugget from Australia

Burning oil in Iran

Chunks like this split away under extremes of heat and cold, combined with moisture from rain and dew

Three wind-polished surfaces

ROCK HARD
Pink granite is one of the hardest rocks and has been used since ancient times: the Egyptians made their splendid obelisks (giant needles) from this rock. It is an igneous rock, which means that it formed when molten rock solidified.

SANDSTONE
Sandstone is simply made of grains of sand which, under pressure, have cemented together. Under a magnifying glass it can be seen that this piece of sandstone was formed in a desert, because the grains have been polished and rounded by the wind.

Desert treasures
Just like other regions of the world, deserts have their fair share of minerals. Oil is one of the most important, found in huge quantities trapped in rocks beneath the deserts of the Middle East. Flares lighting up the desert sky show waste gas being burned off in an Iranian oil field. Oil only became important with the development of motorized transport in the late 19th century, whereas gold has always been highly valued. In Roman times, gold and other valuable goods were carried by camel caravan across the Sahara (p. 38). Today the lure of gold sets miners working in the heat of the Australian Great Sandy Desert.

Rocky deserts

ROCKS IN THE SAHARA
Only one-fifth of the Sahara is covered with sand. The rest is made up of rocky desert, and gravel or stony plains.

As ELSEWHERE, LANDFORMS in the desert begin when rocks are thrust upwards, such as during mountain building. Over millions of years, the rocks are gradually weathered by the effects of heat, cold, wind, rain, and chemical processes. In deserts, the scarce rainfall means that there are few plants to provide a protective cover, so the landscape is angular. When it does rain, it pours, and the torrents and floods are important in shaping the landscape: boulders and stones are carried down temporary rivers, gouging out the bedrock. Wind-borne sand also scours away the rocks to sculpt strange-looking formations. Rocks crack due to the extreme variation in daily temperatures: they expand when heated up under the hot sun, only to contract during the cold nights, which sometimes makes them split with a loud bang. All these processes result in some of the most spectacular rock formations on Earth.

Birds nest in crevices in the rock

BRIDGING THE GAP
A man is standing on a natural sandstone bridge in the Jordanian desert. Bridges and arches are made when rainwater seeps into the rock, loosening particles that are then blasted away by wind-borne sand. Once a hole forms it is made bigger by rock falls and further erosion.

MUSHROOM ROCK
Mushroom rocks come in a variety of shapes and sizes but all have a cap-like top on a narrower base. In a sandstorm, the wind can only bounce along the ground to a height of about 1 m (3 ft). This scours away the base of the rock but not the top. This sandstone mushroom rock in the Jordanian desert is about 8 m (26 ft) high.

Dry cliffs under attack from wind, water, and extreme temperatures

Wind blows the sand into ripples

Plants growing in the desert are spaced apart so that each gets enough water

ROCK PANORAMA
Over millions of years, these rock cliffs in the Jordanian desert will be worn down to make a flat sandy plain. Because of the dry climate, the weathering process takes much longer than in more humid areas. Heaped along the bottom of the cliffs is a skirt of eroded rock which has fallen down from the upper layers of rock.

IN A WADI
The line of plants shows that there is some moisture along the floor of this wadi in Jordan. Wadis are called arroyos in the Americas. It is dangerous to be in wadis when it rains because they fill with torrents of water which sweep away boulders, pebbles, and sand in a churning mass. The walls of the wadi are steep-sided, and they are cut back further with each flood.

GRAND CANYON
One of the natural wonders of the world, the Grand Canyon is 446 km (277 miles) long and cuts through 1.9 km (1.2 miles) of rock in north-west Arizona, USA. At the bottom is the Colorado River, which began to erode the plateau over a million years ago, and continues to erode materials from the river bed. The walls of the canyon show several geological ages, with the oldest rocks at the bottom dating back over 1,600 million years.

Glasswort

Asphodel

PINNACLES
These 2-m (6.5-ft) limestone pinnacles are found in the desert of Western Australia. They were first formed at the roots of plants growing on dunes over 20,000 years ago. Over thousands of years, the limestone dissolved and reformed to create these rock formations, which were revealed when the surrounding soil blew away.

PLANTS OF SAND AND ROCK
Some hardy plants survive all year round in the desert, such as the spiky dry-looking bush which is seen below growing on the sandy Jordanian desert floor. This bush is a kind of glasswort which is a salt-tolerant succulent with scale-like leaves. The asphodel grows among rocks and compacted soils. It has an underground tuber (swollen root) for food storage.

The desert floor is gravelly sand

Layers of rock are easy to see without plant cover

Wind-blown sand collects around the base of plants

Seas of sand

NOTHING CAPTURES THE ROMANCE of the desert more than the great sand seas with their endless stretches of beautiful dunes. The largest continuous expanse of sand is the infamous Empty Quarter, part of the Arabian Desert, which covers 647,500 sq km (250,000 sq miles). The huge quantities of sand that make sandy deserts were originally eroded from mountains and highlands. The sand was carried by rivers or floods to the lowlands where it was picked up by the winds and dropped in the desert. Some desert sand also comes from the shores of lakes and seas. Winds blow dunes into a variety of shapes; some shapes, such as the star dune, are quite stable, while others, such as the barchan dune, shift as much as 20 m (66 ft) a year.

These are clicking sticks, used in ritual dances to make music

SAND ART
Some Aboriginal peoples from the Australian deserts traditionally drew totemic images in the sand as part of their beliefs. Today some of the images are made permanent by using acrylic paints. Some of these dot paintings are sold to the art market but sacred symbols are never included. These artefacts were painted by the Napaljarri people.

Wind flows over mound of sand

Crest gradually builds up

Eventually the crest of the dune may collapse like an ocean wave

MAKING A DUNE
Sand is carried by the wind for short distances, but even the strongest wind only lifts sand grains about 1 m (3 ft) off the ground. A sand dune begins to form where there is an obstacle, such as a plant, which slows down the wind and makes it drop its load of sand. As the sand accumulates, it forms a bigger barrier to the wind, causing more sand to be dropped.

GLORIOUS SAND
The Namib Desert is one of the oldest in the world, dating back 55 million years or more. Beneath the modern dunes (shown here) are ancient dunes some 40 million years old. Both ancient and modern dunes are formed from sands carried from the nearby coast by strong winds. The sand originally came from highlands far away and was carried by a river out to the sea and then washed ashore. Some dunes in the Namib reach 244 m (800 ft) in height.

As the body dries out, it shrinks

The very dry conditions prevent the body decaying

NATURAL MUMMY
Burying a dead body in dry desert sand is enough to preserve it. Such simple burials took place in Egypt about 5,000 years ago. The body was placed in a shallow grave with a few possessions and covered with sand. As the body dried out it turned into a mummy. Later on, when burials became more complex, the internal organs were removed and the body wrapped in bandages, because it did not dry out as well as in a sand grave.

RIDGE DUNES
Where there is plenty of sand, and winds blowing in one direction, parallel ridges of sand form. As the ridges are at right angles to the wind, they are called transverse dunes.

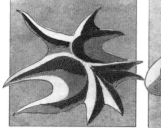

STAR DUNES
Star-shaped dunes form where the direction of the wind shifts so that it comes from several directions. In some deserts, star dunes reach 80 m (260 ft) high. There are many star dunes in the sand seas of the Sahara Desert.

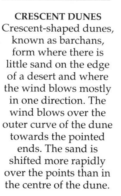

CRESCENT DUNES
Crescent-shaped dunes, known as barchans, form where there is little sand on the edge of a desert and where the wind blows mostly in one direction. The wind blows over the outer curve of the dune towards the pointed ends. The sand is shifted more rapidly over the points than in the centre of the dune.

SAND BARRIERS
Shifting sand is threatening a desert oasis. While barriers help to hold back wind-blown sand, villages and oases sometimes become completely covered over with sand.

SEA OF SAND
Tuareg warriors are about to cross a sea of sand dunes. Desert peoples, such as the Tuareg, have an uncanny ability to find their way through what to others would be a featureless expanse of sand. Getting lost in the desert can be a fatal mistake.

Water in the desert

Azraq oasis in Jordan is shrinking because of the amount of water pumped out

SOME PARTS OF THE DESERT are not dry and barren: occasional rainfall turns pockets of the desert green and fills dry riverbeds with floods of water. Some of this water is trapped behind small dams or, after it has seeped away, is tapped by digging wells into the riverbed. Water from deep layers of rock comes to the surface at oases, where crops such as date palms are cultivated. With the help of various irrigation methods, the water spreads further, so more of the desert can be cultivated. Today vast areas of the desert are green as a result of pumping water from deep bore wells. But there is a danger that underground water may run dry, especially when more people settle in the desert and when crops needing a large amount of water are grown.

BUCKET AND POLE
Water is taken from a well using a shaduf. The bucket on the long pole is lowered into a well to fill it, then swung up with the help of the counter-weight on the end of the long pole.

RAIN NECKLACE
The figure on this Zuni necklace represents a shalako, a messenger of the rain-makers. People dressed as shalakos and wearing masks take part in a special ceremony.

WATER WHEEL
Water is drawn up by a water wheel at an Egyptian oasis. The cow is blindfolded so that it will walk around in a circle turning the big spoked wheel. As this wheel turns it drives the water-wheel around, filling the metal buckets. The water pours out of the buckets into an irrigation channel to water the crops. In the past, clay pots would have been used instead of metal buckets.

Water in aquifer (porous rock)

Impermeable rock

Oasis

Water flows up fault to oasis

Tail parts

A series of limbs are used to push food into their mouths

View from below of tadpole shrimp

Tadpole shrimps are 3 cm (1.5 in) long

Shield covering head and front of trunk

Eyes

WATER FROM FAR AWAY
Rain falling on mountains seeps through into permeable rocks. The water comes to the surface at an oasis where a fault (split) in the rock layers blocks its passage. Rocks that hold water are known as aquifers. Wells are often drilled through the rocks to reach aquifer water. The water contained in an aquifer may be rain which fell thousands of years ago.

BABY DAM
To hold the water that drains from these Jordanian cliffs during rain, the Bedouin have built a small dam. The water is for their own use as well as for their livestock. In places where there are water supplies, the Bedouin may live a more settled existence.

Top view of a tadpole shrimp

THIRSTY SHRIMPS
The eggs of these tadpole shrimps survive in dry sands for ten years or more before rain comes to bring them to life. The shrimps must grow quickly to reach maturity and produce eggs before the desert pool in which they live dries up and they die.

The cobra only sees movements, not shapes

Windpipe enables the cobra to breathe while swallowing its prey

SPITTING COBRA

The red spitting cobra lurks in palm groves at oases in eastern Africa. If disturbed, it usually tries to escape, but if it is provoked any further, it rears up and spits toxic venom, which can hit a target at least 2 m (6.5 feet) away. If the venom hits an animal or a person in the eye it is extremely painful, and if untreated can cause blindness. The venom is ejected from tiny holes in the fangs at the front of the mouth. This cobra eats lizards, toads, snakes, birds, and small mammals.

WATER ON THE WAY

Water from an oasis is sent on its way to water palms through a series of channels. Some channels are permanent, like this one in Oman; others are confined in mud banks which are broken and rebuilt to send the water in different directions. Palms do not need to be irrigated if there is enough ground water close to the surface. They provide dates to eat, wood for building, leaves for thatching and fencing, and fibres to make rope.

Enlarged glands secrete a strong poison to deter predators

GREEN TOAD

Green toads live at oases where there is a permanent water supply in which to lay their eggs. During the day they hide under stones; at night they come out to hunt insects near water holes and around palm trees.

GREENING THE DESERT

An aerial view shows giant green crop circles on the fringes of the Sahara Desert in Morocco. The circles are made by sprinkler systems which rotate like the hands of a watch. Huge quantities of water pumped up from underground are used to keep crops, such as wheat, growing in the desert. While these crops provide much-needed food, there is a danger that the water from aquifers is used up much faster than it is replaced.

After the rains

SOME PLANTS AND ANIMALS SURVIVE in the desert by avoiding the driest times, only growing or becoming active after occasional rains. Plants exist in the dry soil for years as seeds. When the rains come, it can take several good soakings before the seeds germinate. This prevents seeds germinating unless there is enough water for them to flower and produce seeds. The eggs of desert crustaceans, such as brine and tadpole shrimps (p. 14), also need water to bring them to life. Not all the eggs hatch the first time round. Some eggs are left for the next rains, in case the pools dry out and the first batch of shrimp die before they complete their life cycle. Spadefoot toads face a similar problem, so not all breed after the first rains. In the dry season, the toads remain inactive, buried in the soil. They come out as soon as they hear the drumming of rain on the surface.

BRINE SHRIMP
Brine shrimp live in salt lakes and pools around the world. During dry periods these lakes evaporate, and the brine shrimp die, leaving eggs behind. Some of the eggs are drought resistant and can withstand high temperatures. They remain viable for decades.

JUST ADD WATER
Within 48 hours of a rainfall, the dormant eggs of the brine shrimp hatch out into larvae (young forms). These feed on small food particles in the water and grow, like all crustaceans, by shedding their outer skeletons.

ADD LEGS
The young shrimps go through several moults, adding more pairs of legs. The length of the life cycle depends on the temperature of the water and the amount of food available; brine shrimp can reach maturity about three weeks after hatching.

ADD EGGS
Adult shrimps are quick to mate to produce eggs before the lake dries up. A female can produce 140 eggs in a single batch and she can live for four months laying eggs every four days.

ADULT SHRIMP
Brine shrimps are less than 1 cm (0.4 in) long. They are an important food for birds visiting salt lakes. Brine shrimps are tolerant of a wide range of salt concentrations, from nearly fresh water to water five times as salty as sea water.

BLOOMS IN THE NEGEV
This member of the daisy family only grows in good years when there is enough rain in the Negev Desert in Israel. Plants grow along the edge of gulleys where rain collects but cannot survive in the gulleys where they would be washed away. The leaves have a strong smell because they contain oils which deter grazing animals.

DESERT PEA
The bold flowers of Sturt's desert pea add to the blooms which carpet parts of the central deserts of Australia after good rains. Sturt's desert pea rambles along the ground for several metres. By the time the ground dries up again the pea has already produced seeds which will spring to life with the next rains.

DESERT LILY
This desert lily blooms in the deserts of the south-west USA from March to May. The lily shoots up each year from a bulb underground after the rains. It can grow up to 1.8 m (5.9 ft) tall. The bulbs were once used by the Native Americans for food.

LITTLE SNAPDRAGON VINE
Seeds of the snapdragon vine from the Chihuahuan and Sonoran Deserts germinate after the rains. The long vines curl around other desert plants. In the colder winter months the vine dies back in to the sand or gravelly soil. Snapdragon vines also grow in juniper forests.

*Flowers are
pollinated by
visiting insects
so that seeds can develop
for next year's plants*

*In the dry season the
toads live off their fat
reserves and water
stored in their bladder*

SPADEFOOT TOAD

Spadefoot toads spend most of their lives buried
in the deserts of the south-west USA. When it
rains, they dig themselves out and head for
temporary pools to they mate and lay their
eggs. The eggs hatch into tadpoles which
develop into toadlets in less than 10 days.
Most tadpoles feed on plants and dead animals,
but a few are carnivores and grow more quickly by
feeding on other animals, including smaller toads.

GIANT RED VELVET MITE

The largest of the mites, giant red velvet mites are
about the size of a berry, 1.6 cm (0.6 in) long. They
come to the surface after rain to feed on termites,
which swarm at this time. The bright red colour
is a warning that these mites do not taste good,
so potential predators
avoid them.

*The snapdragon
vine can grow up
to 2 m (6.5 ft) long*

*After the flower
has been fertilized,
it withers, and
seeds are produced*

*Leaves make food by
photosynthesis for
plant to flower and
produce seeds quickly*

DESERT IN BLOOM

Namaqualand, on the southern
fringes of the Namib Desert in
south-west Africa, is famous for its
fabulous show of spring flowers that
cover the ground after the rains.

How plants survive in the desert

Pᴌᴀɴᴛꜱ ᴛʜᴀᴛ ʟɪᴠᴇ ɪɴ ᴅᴇꜱᴇʀᴛꜱ either spring up from seeds after rain (pp. 16–17), or stay alive all year by adapting to the meagre supply of water. These more permanent plants have a variety of ways to get water. Some have long roots to reach water deep in the soil, some spread their roots to collect water over a wide area, and some can absorb dew through their leaves. Many desert plants, including cacti, are succulents that are able to store water. A thick waxy layer on the stems and leaves helps retain this water and protects tissues from intense sunshine. Reducing leaf size, shedding leaves in times of drought, or even having no leaves at all, also help to reduce water loss by keeping the surface area of the plant to a minimum.

DATE PALMS
A grove of date palms cultivated at an oasis in Oman (p. 15). Only female trees produce dates, so only a few male trees are grown to produce pollen. Palm trees can live for up to 200 years.

FRESH DATES
There are many different varieties of dates. Most familiar are the ones that are dried and packed in boxes for export around the world. Dried dates are also part of the staple diet of villagers and desert nomads such as the Bedouin. They are highly nutritious and do not rot.

FLESHY LEAF
Haworthias grow in places with some shade, next to rocks or other plants. Only the tip of the leaves poke above the surface of the soil, to keep the rest out of the sun. But leaves need light to be able to make food by photosynthesis. This leaf has a translucent (clear) window in the tip to allow light through the leaf. In times of drought, this species shrinks into the ground.

Very long roots to seek out water

These variegated agaves have been specially bred

CENTURY PLANTS *above left*
It takes 20 to 50 years for the century plant to produce flowers on a stem up to 9 m (30 ft) tall which grows out of the centre of the plant. The flowers are pollinated by nectar-seeking bats. After flowering and producing seeds the plant dies. The century plant belongs to the agave family, members of which are a source of sweet sap for drinks, and fibres for ropes and other products.

FIRE THORN BRANCH
Also called the ocotillo or coachwhip plant, the fire thorn grows in the deserts of south-west USA. In dry times, it sheds its leaves to conserve moisture. After rains, new leaves grow among the spines; if the ground is wet enough, the fire thorn flowers.

WELWITSCHIA
This bizarre plant has only two frayed strap-like leaves, and a huge tap root which may be up to 1 m (3 ft) wide at the top. It grows on the gravel plains in the Namib Desert. Welwitschia is actually a dwarf tree, and may live for a thousand years or more.

Welwitschia leaves usually split into many strips

Leaf absorbs dew

When spread out, each leaf reaches up to 2 m (6.5 ft) long

INSIDE A CACTUS

Cut open a cactus and inside is a mass of water-storing tissue. The vascular or transport tissue, called xylem, not only transports water from the roots but also helps to support the plant. The surface of the cactus is covered with a thick waxy layer which helps prevent loss of water and protects the tissue from the burning effects of the sun.

BARREL CACTUS

A cactus is well adapted to make the most of any water available (p. 20, p. 36). Their shallow roots spread out around the plant to absorb moisture from rain or dew. Desert cacti open their stomata (pores) at night to exchange gases for respiration and photosynthesis instead of during the day like most plants. This reduces the amount of water lost through the stomata. Cacti store carbon dioxide taken in for photosynthesis in another chemical form until it is ready to be used during daylight.

LIFE-GIVING DEW

Dew from the coastal fog (p. 6) has settled on a salt bush in the Namib Desert. For plants and animals dew is a vital source of water. Some shrubs are coated with salt, and this is thought to help the plant take in more moisture from the fog.

LIVING STONES

Stone plants are often hard to spot as they are so well camouflaged; this saves them from plant-eating animals. Stone plants are succulents – they store water in their leaves. They grow with all but the tips of their leaves in the ground, and the surrounding soil and stones protect them from intense sunlight. To allow light to reach the underground part of the leaf, the surface of the leaf tips have translucent (clear) windows. After rains, stone plants bloom, producing a single large flower between the leaf pair. They grow in southern Africa.

NOT FAIR

This spike of flowers in the Jordanian desert belongs to the leafless cistanche plant. It does not need green leaves for photosynthesis (the manufacture of food from carbon dioxide and water using sunlight) because it taps the roots of other plants for food. Living organisms that steal food and harm their hosts are called parasites.

Continued on next page

Cacti and other succulents

Succulents are plants that survive dry conditions by storing water in their fleshy stems or leaves. Cacti are the best-known succulents, with their bizarre-shaped stems varying from globes growing close to the ground to tall skyward-pointing branched forms. They are mainly found growing wild in the Americas but are not restricted to deserts. Other desert succulents show a great variety of forms, including some which look remarkably like cacti.

Yellow flowers are followed by smooth green fruits, which are eaten by birds; they then disperse the seeds

AGAVE CACTUS
A cactus plant that looks rather like an agave (p. 18), the agave cactus is found in the dry regions and grasslands of Mexico. This cactus grows to 70 cm (28 in), and it has a tap root which grows to 30 cm (12 in) to reach water.

Cultivated forms are often grafted on to other cacti, to make them grow better

KOKERBOOM TREE
This tree aloe, which grows in drylands of southwest Africa, can survive several years of drought, during which time its leaves shrink, having lost most of their sap. The kokerboom tree grows several metres tall. Its wood was once used by the San to make arrows (p. 46).

Kokerboom tree in the wild

DESERT ROSE
A succulent which grows among rocks in drylands of Africa through to the Arabian Peninsula, the desert rose has a poisonous milky sap to deter animals from eating it. In good conditions, the desert rose grows over 2 m (6.5 ft) high. It can flower in the dry season even when it has no leaves.

SILVER DOLLAR
One of the most beautiful cacti, the silver dollar is under threat of extinction, as are many desert plants, due to people stealing them from the wild even though some are cultivated for sale in nurseries. The silver dollar grows in the southern USA and northern Mexico among rocks, sand, and bushes.

LIVING ROCK
Looking like a rock may help this spineless cactus avoid being eaten by some animals, but it is devoured by goats. It grows among rocks in southern USA and northern Mexico.

CACTUS DRUG

The mescal or peyote cactus contains the drug mescaline. Since the times of the Aztecs (the ancient Mexicans), this cactus has been gathered from the wild and eaten raw, dried, or consumed as a drink for its hallucinogenic properties. Only the top of the cactus is collected, leaving the large roots in the ground so the cactus regrows. Collection in the USA and Mexico is now banned.

The saguaro reaches over 12 m (39 ft) in height

The giant saguaro has shallow roots for gathering water, and deeper roots to anchor it in the ground

PRICKLY PEAR

One of the better-known kinds of cactus, prickly pears have been introduced to many parts of the world. This Texas prickly pear is a popular garden plant in the southern USA. Prickly pears position their leaf-like lobes (pads) in such a way as to cut down on exposure to the sun. This helps them keep cool.

This cactus is sometimes called fishhook cactus because of its spines

GIANT HOME

A giant saguaro from the desert of the south-west USA and Mexico provides a home for a variety of animals (p. 31), rather like a skyscraper. Like many permanent desert plants it grows slowly: it can take over 40 years for the saguaro to put out a branch. The side of the plant facing the strongest sun has a thicker wax layer to protect it from being burnt. It may hold several tonnes of water in its swollen stems.

CANDY CACTUS

The white inner tissue of this barrel cactus was once cut into small cubes to make candy. The cubes were boiled in water first to get rid of any bitter taste, then boiled in syrup before being rolled in sugar and left to dry in the sun. Collection in the wild is banned.

WHISKER CACTUS

When this plant starts to mature, the spines at the tip of the stems become long and curly, and look like whiskers. This is when the pink flowers appear, and they are followed by red berries. The flowers open at night, so that insects, such as moths, can feed on the nectar.

Top view of hedgehog cactus

HEDGEHOG CACTUS

Hedgehog cacti are named for their prickly set of spines. This one is found in North American deserts, from the Great Basin Desert in the north to the Chihuahuan Desert in the south. It grows about 15 cm (6 in) high on rocky slopes, and produces brightly coloured flowers after rain.

NOT A CACTUS

This cactus-like euphorbia comes from the fringes of the Arabian desert. Many euphorbias living in dry regions look like cacti, although they are not related to them. Both cacti and these euphorbias have evolved similar ways to cope with drought by not having leaves, and storing water in their fleshy stems.

Insects

HONEY-POT ANT
This honey-pot ant's abdomen is so swollen with nectar and other sugary substances that it cannot move and stays anchored to the nest ceiling. Ants like this one serve to feed the nest. Honey-pot ants are found in North America, southern Africa, and Australia, where they are one of the traditional foods of some of the Aboriginal peoples of the central deserts.

INSECTS HAVE ADAPTED to almost every environment in the world, so it is not surprising to find them living in deserts. Like other desert animals, insects face the problem of finding enough food and water. Some plant-eating insects, such as the caterpillar stage of butterflies, feed on the fresh green plants that spring up after rain. They survive the dry times either as eggs or as pupae (the stage in which the caterpillar turns into a butterfly). Seed-eaters, such as harvester ants, store seeds to last them through the drought, while honey-pot ants store sugary substances within the bodies of some of their nest mates. Hunting insects get some moisture from their prey. Dew is an important source of water for many insects, and some beetles even have special ways to collect it. To avoid the drying effects of the sun, many desert insects only come out at night.

Like all insects, the jewel wasp has a pair of antennae on its head

Ant lion adult

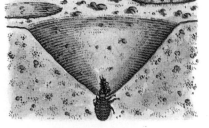

JEWEL WASP
A jewel wasp takes a drink. Jewel wasps are one of the solitary wasps that live on their own instead of in colonies. The adults feed on nectar from flowers, but their young devour cockroaches caught for them by the adult female. She hunts down the cockroach, stings it to paralyse it, and then drags it into a hole where she lays an egg on it. When the young hatches from the egg it feeds on the paralysed but live cockroach.

HARVESTER ANTS
These industrious ants collect seeds to store in granaries in their nests. When a scout ant finds a rich supply of seeds, it trails a special odour from the tip of its abdomen all the way back to the nest. Nest mates then follow the trail out to the seeds to collect them for the nest. The ants eat most of the seeds, but they do reject or drop a few, and therefore help plants by dispersing the seeds.

ANT LION
The larva (young) of this winged insect is called an ant lion. As soon as it hatches, it digs a pit in the sand and hides at the bottom with only its jaws exposed, waiting for an insect, perhaps an ant, to come into the pit. When an insect does, the ant lion flicks sand at it so that it loses its footing and slides down to be snapped up by the deadly jaws.

*Jointed legs end
in claws for
gripping surfaces*

*Abdomen points
upwards so that dew
runs into mouth*

*Shiny outer skeleton
which gives the jewel
wasp its name*

*Two pairs
of wings*

BEETLE IN A HEAD-STAND

Moisture in the early morning fog in
the Namib Desert has condensed on this
darkling beetle's back; the dew then runs
down into its mouth. This is the only way
this beetle gets a drink. It spends the night
buried in sand, but should there be a night-
time fog, it will come to the surface. Dew-
collecting beetles also live in other deserts,
such as the Wahiba Sands in the southern
Arabian Peninsula, where there is coastal
fog and high dew fall. Some darkling
beetles make little furrows in the
sand or small hummocks
to collect dew.

*Darkling beetle
straightens its
legs to run along
on hot sand*

*The hard wing cases
are stuck together, so
this beetle cannot fly*

*White spots are a warning that
the domino beetle is armed and
does not taste good*

DARKLING BEETLE

This beetle lives in the Namib Desert, where it feeds on
wind-blown plant debris and seeds on the surface of
the sand dunes. It is an unusual kind of darkling
beetle in that it has all-white wing cases. These
may reflect the heat and allow the beetle to
stay out in the sun finding food for
longer than black beetles.

DOMINO BEETLE

The white spots on domino beetles'
backs are a warning that these
beetles are armed with chemical
weapons. When threatened, they
squirt a jet of acid at an attacker.
After this, the attacker will be unlikely to
try to eat a beetle with white spots again.
During the day, domino beetles lurk under
rocks and holes made by other animals.
They come out at night to hunt insects and
other small prey. This domino beetle lives
in the drylands of northern Africa
through to the Middle East.

Insects and arachnids

Winged insects, such as locusts, are able to fly to new places to find food and to breed. Swarming locusts are nomads, flying from place to place to find enough plants to eat. Some insects, such as moths, lay their eggs on the food source so that when their wingless young hatch out they do not need to move far to find food. Scorpions and their relatives, the camel-spiders and whip scorpions, are all arachnids – a group that includes true spiders and mites (p. 17). Arachnids do not have wings but some, such as the camel-spider, can run fast.

Then the locust opens its wings and starts to fly

To take off the locust jumps with its wings closed, so that it can leap as high as possible

LOCUST LAUNCH
Locusts, just like other grasshoppers, have strong back legs which they flex to leap into the air. The muscles lie inside the outer skeleton of the legs and are a thousand times stronger than the same weight of human muscle. Once airborne, the locust opens its wings and starts to fly using both pairs of wings. Locusts can fly long distances at speeds of about 35 km/h (22 mph), both flying and being carried in the wind.

SAHARA SCORPION
Scorpions only sting if they are cornered or stepped on accidentally. The sting of this 7-cm (2.8-in) scorpion is strong enough to kill a person. Scorpions also use their stings to kill prey, which include insects and spiders. They get enough moisture from their prey and do not need to drink. During the day they hide in burrows, or, like this species, under rocks.

Claws for holding prey

DISAPPEARING ACT
This desert cricket from India and Pakistan can disappear into sand in seconds by using its feet to dig a hole directly beneath it. The ends of the wings are coiled up to keep them out of the way. They can also unfurl these wings and fly well.

Star-shaped feet help the cricket to bury itself in sand

FIERCE FIGHT
The contest between a camel-spider and a scorpion is closely matched because the camel-spider is armed with huge jaws while the scorpion defends itself with its powerful sting. If a camel-spider were struck by the scorpion's sting it would die within a few minutes, but in practice the camel-spider usually wins.

Like all arachnids, camel-spiders have four pairs of walking legs

Long antennae

24

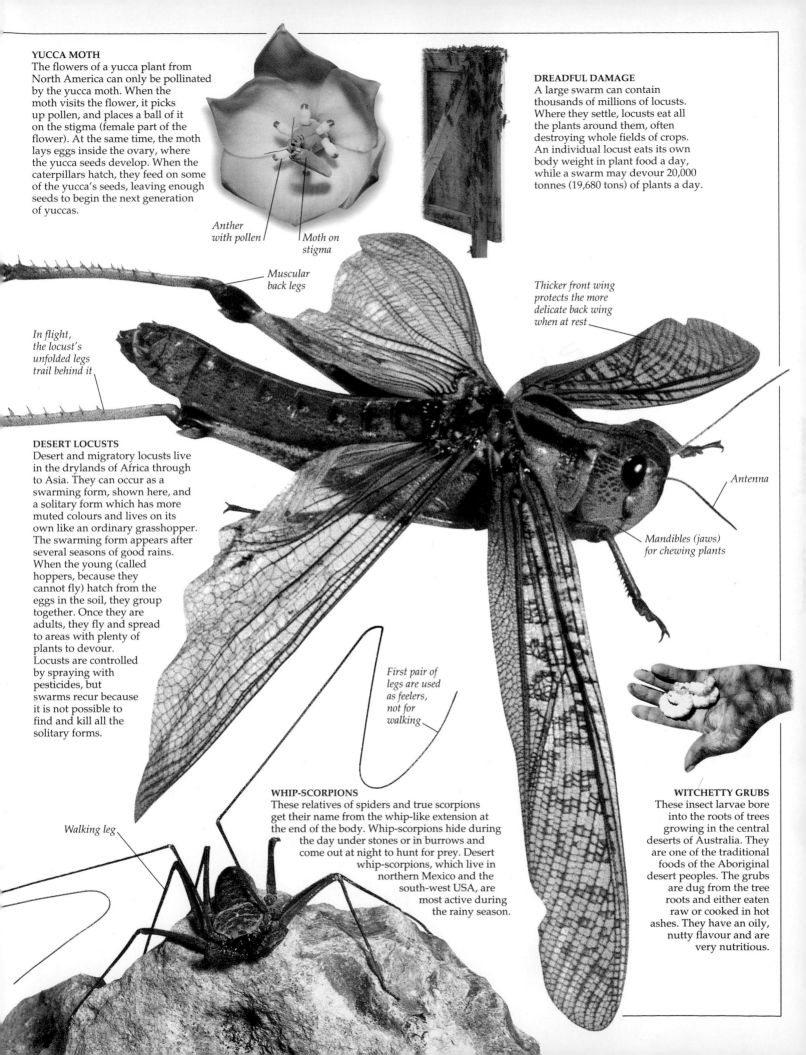

YUCCA MOTH
The flowers of a yucca plant from North America can only be pollinated by the yucca moth. When the moth visits the flower, it picks up pollen, and places a ball of it on the stigma (female part of the flower). At the same time, the moth lays eggs inside the ovary, where the yucca seeds develop. When the caterpillars hatch, they feed on some of the yucca's seeds, leaving enough seeds to begin the next generation of yuccas.

Anther with pollen

Moth on stigma

DREADFUL DAMAGE
A large swarm can contain thousands of millions of locusts. Where they settle, locusts eat all the plants around them, often destroying whole fields of crops. An individual locust eats its own body weight in plant food a day, while a swarm may devour 20,000 tonnes (19,680 tons) of plants a day.

Muscular back legs

Thicker front wing protects the more delicate back wing when at rest

In flight, the locust's unfolded legs trail behind it

DESERT LOCUSTS
Desert and migratory locusts live in the drylands of Africa through to Asia. They can occur as a swarming form, shown here, and a solitary form which has more muted colours and lives on its own like an ordinary grasshopper. The swarming form appears after several seasons of good rains. When the young (called hoppers, because they cannot fly) hatch from the eggs in the soil, they group together. Once they are adults, they fly and spread to areas with plenty of plants to devour. Locusts are controlled by spraying with pesticides, but swarms recur because it is not possible to find and kill all the solitary forms.

Antenna

Mandibles (jaws) for chewing plants

First pair of legs are used as feelers, not for walking

Walking leg

WHIP-SCORPIONS
These relatives of spiders and true scorpions get their name from the whip-like extension at the end of the body. Whip-scorpions hide during the day under stones or in burrows and come out at night to hunt for prey. Desert whip-scorpions, which live in northern Mexico and the south-west USA, are most active during the rainy season.

WITCHETTY GRUBS
These insect larvae bore into the roots of trees growing in the central deserts of Australia. They are one of the traditional foods of the Aboriginal desert peoples. The grubs are dug from the tree roots and either eaten raw or cooked in hot ashes. They have an oily, nutty flavour and are very nutritious.

Reptiles

REPTILES, such as snakes, lizards (pp. 28–29), and tortoises, do well in deserts because they control their body temperature by gaining or losing heat from their surroundings. By using external sources of heat, reptiles do not expend so much energy compared to birds and mammals, which generate heat within their bodies. So reptiles need less food, a scarce commodity in deserts. Using less energy also means that reptiles do not breathe as frequently as birds and mammals do, and this helps them conserve moisture. Compared to amphibians, such as toads, with their permeable skins, reptiles are better suited to the desert because they have a scaly skin to help them conserve moisture.

Black band marks the position of the hood, which is only extended when the cobra feels threatened or curious

TORTOISE BAG
A bag made from a tortoise shell that was used to carry scented ointment by Herero women from Namibia. Tortoises are slow breeders, and if too many are killed they will be threatened with extinction.

TONGUE OUT
Like all snakes, the diadem snake uses its tongue to pick up scents from the air and the ground. The scents are transferred to a sensory organ in the roof of the mouth which detects chemicals. The snake does this to find out what is going on around it.

SPITTING COBRA
The red spitting cobra spreads its hood before spitting venom (p. 15) to defend itself. When attacking its prey, mainly small reptiles and mammals, the cobra bites to inject venom. Like many desert snakes, it hunts at night to avoid the heat of the day.

BRIGHT EYES
The grey banded kingsnake has big eyes which help it hunt for prey at night. It feeds mainly on lizards but also eats snakes and small mammals. Like all snakes, it seems to stare because it does not have proper eyelids and does not blink: a transparent scale protects its eyes. This snake lives in desert scrub from south Texas, USA to Mexico.

TAKE IT EASY
The desert tortoise from the southern USA and Mexican deserts avoids the heat of the day by staying in its burrow. It comes out during the early morning and late afternoon to feed on plants and is partial to red and orange flowers. The desert tortoise takes 15 years or more to reach maturity.

If caught out in hot sun, under severe heat stress the desert tortoise will empty its bladder over its back legs to cool down, while saliva froths over its head and neck

LEAVE ME ALONE

Rattlesnakes warn enemies off by rattling the hollow segments of skin at the tip of their tails. This does not use up water as hissing does. If provoked further, they may strike. Rattlesnakes such as this western diamondback have front fangs that swing forward to inject venom.

BLACK RATTLER

Western rattlesnakes (from the western USA) come in a number of different colours. This black version lives in the more mountainous areas of desert in Arizona. Western rattlesnakes living in these areas and the Great Basin Desert group together in a communal den during the cold winter.

SNAKE HEADS

The desert kingsnake has a characteristic black mask covering its head. Reaching 1.5 m (5 ft) long, it can kill rattlesnakes two-thirds of its own length. Kingsnakes kill their prey by constriction, wrapping their body around the victim's. The lyre snake restrains its prey by constriction, and injects weak venom from fangs at the back of its jaw. Its eyes have slit-shaped pupils which open up at night, just like a cat's, to help it see in the dark to hunt lizards, mice, and bats in their roosts. The milksnake's bright colours may mimic the colours of the highly venomous coral snakes. Wary of these colours, animals will leave the harmless milk-snake alone.

Desert kingsnake from the southern USA and northern Mexico

Lyre snake from the coastal desert of southern California, USA and northern Baja California, Mexico

Red spitting cobra from desert and oases in eastern Africa

HOGNOSE

These snakes are named for their snouts. This one lives in deserts and prairies in the USA and Mexico. It feeds on small mammals, and reptiles and their eggs. When threatened, a hognose snake hisses loudly and flattens its head and neck. If the attacker persists, the snake rolls over with its tongue out and pretends to be dead, hoping that it will be left alone.

Sinaloan milksnake from desert fringes and other habitats in western Mexico

Bright colours may also confuse or startle a predator

Overlapping belly scales allow for rapid and agile movement

Continued on next page

Lizards

Lizards are more numerous in deserts than snakes, and they are easier to spot because they are often active during the day, whereas many snakes are secretive and only active at night. Many lizards like to bask in the sun in the early morning to warm up their muscles after a cold desert night. In the heat of the day, they retreat into the shade of rocks or plants, down cool burrows, or even clamber into bushes. Most desert lizards change colour to blend into their backgrounds to avoid being seen by predators. Spiny skins make some desert lizards more unpalatable. When threatened, some lizards put on intimidating displays with gaping jaws. Biting an attacker is always an option but many lizards prefer to run away.

FRINGE-TOED LIZARD

This fast-moving lizard can run across the surface of sand dunes in the Sahara desert, where it lives. It has a fringe of scales on its feet which act like snow shoes to spread its weight so that it does not sink into the sand. To stay cooler on hot sand, it holds its head and body clear of the surface. The nostrils have valves which close to prevent sand getting into its air passages.

Fringe of scales on toe

In places, the scales form spines

BEARDED DRAGON

A formidable-looking lizard, the bearded dragon from the dry interior of Australia has spiny skin to protect itself from predators. The beard under the chin can be expanded to make the dragon look even more scary. Dragons feed on a variety of food including insects, bird eggs, newborn small mammals, and some dew-soaked plants. Bearded dragons are active in the early morning and late afternoon. During the heat of the day, they often climb into shrubs where it is cooler.

It is the layer of skin under the scales that changes colour

Bearded dragons are darker in the morning to absorb the heat of the sun, and get paler as the day wears on

HORNED TOAD

Despite its name, this is a lizard, not a toad, and it lives in North American deserts. It often sits in the open eating ants, as its pale colours help it blend in with its desert background, making it difficult to spot. Horned toads also lower their bodies close to the ground to get rid of any tell-tale shadows. The spiny skin is another line of defence. If attacked, horned toads can squirt blood from their eyes to put off an attacker.

Colours warn this animal is poisonous

As in the spiny-tailed lizard, the tail is also a fat store

Chameleons are excellent climbers, using their tails and opposing toes to grip plants

GILA MONSTER

The Gila monster is one of only two lizards in the world with a venomous bite. The bite is seldom fatal to humans but causes immense pain. The Gila monster lives in scrub in the Mojave and Sonoran Deserts. Gila monsters are mainly active at night, feeding on small mammals, snakes, and other lizards.

HEADS OR TAILS?

The shingleback from the Australian deserts has a fat, head-shaped tail which makes it hard for a predator to know which end to attack. If a predator attacks its tail instead of the vulnerable head, the shingleback turns round and bites its attacker. Shinglebacks eat a wide variety of food, including insects, snails, and fruit.

CHAMELEON

A chameleon sits on the stem of a welwitschia plant (p. 18) growing in the Namib Desert. Chameleons and other lizards are attracted to the plant because insects like to shelter under the shade of its leaves. Chameleons catch the insects by shooting out their long, sticky-tipped tongues.

Tail also serves as a fat reserve

LIZARD EGGS
These eggs belong to the eyed lizard from northern Africa. Up to 20 eggs are laid in sandy soil and they hatch two to three months later. Eyed lizards are over 60 cm (2 ft) long. These large lizards feed on insects. small mammals, and other reptiles.

SPINY-TAILED OR DAB LIZARD
One of the hardiest desert lizards from the Sahara, the African spiny-tailed lizard tolerates high temperatures and survives on small amounts of water from dew, and from plants and a few insects that it eats. This lizard is active in the day but avoids the mid-day heat by staying in its deep burrow. If pursued, the lizard runs into a rocky crevice and blocks the exit with its spiny tail. The energy reserve in its fat tail also helps the lizard to endure drought when plants are scarce.

THORNY DEVIL
A spiny body helps to protect this lizard from being attacked. It lives in deserts in Australia, and has a similar ant-eating lifestyle to horned toads. Thorny devils collect rain or dew on their backs, which finds its way down tiny channels into their mouths. These lizards are also known as molochs.

FIERCE FRILLS
The frilled lizard from the Australian desert fringes spreads out a frill around its neck which makes it look larger to scare away enemies. The frill is supported by rods (like an umbrella's) which are attached to a bone at the base of the tongue. When the lizard is angry, it opens its jaws wide, and this automatically spreads the frill. If the pursuer does not retreat, the lizard will charge and bite.

The collared lizard can inflict a nasty bite with its sharp teeth

COLLARED LIZARD
In a defensive pose, the collared lizard opens its mouth in a wide gape. If molested, the lizard will bite. In preference to biting an attacker it will leap away over the rocks where it lives in the deserts of southern USA. The collared lizard is an active predator itself. It hunts during the day for insects, smaller lizards, and even small snakes and mice. Highly agile, it can even leap into the air to catch flying insects.

Sharp claws for gripping rocks

Birds

A VARIETY OF BIRDS live in deserts. Some, such as the tiny elf owl, are permanent residents, while others, such as the galah, are visitors in search of food. Flesh-eating birds, such as falcons, do not need to drink as they get enough moisture from their prey, whereas seed-eating birds, such as sandgrouse, have such a dry diet that they need to drink daily. Because there is so little vegetation, desert birds are restricted in the number of places they can nest. Many birds, such as ostriches, nest on the ground, but their young are vulnerable to attack. Others, such as roadrunners, nest in low bushes, while woodpeckers nest in holes in cacti. Where possible, birds seek out patches of shade. For some, flying at high altitudes means escape from the desert heat. Birds have a higher body temperature than mammals, so they can tolerate higher temperatures. They do not sweat; instead they pant or flutter their throats so that water evaporates from their air passages to help them cool down.

FINE FEATHERED FALCON

With its wing feathers spread, the lanner falcon is poised to strike. Lanner falcons in the Sahara Desert hunt around water holes for sandgrouse. They spot their prey from a great height and then swoop down to catch it in mid-air or on the ground. The falcons' sharp talons grip the prey while their hooked beaks rip the flesh. Lanner falcons also catch lizards and feed on swarming locusts on the ground (p. 25). Because of their superb hunting skills, they are popular birds to train for falconry. Lanner falcons lay three to four eggs on the rocky ledges of desert cliffs.

GALAH

The galah is a cockatoo from Australia. Galahs pair for life, returning to the same nest hole in a tree every year. They regulate their breeding according to conditions, laying as many as five eggs in good years and only one, two, or none in drought years. The chicks hatch out helpless and are fed regurgitated seeds. After the breeding season, galahs disperse to wherever they can find seeds, bulbs, and fruit. They have strong beaks for crushing their food. Galahs are good fliers: large flocks of 100 or more birds can travel over 100 km (60 miles) in a day.

ROADRUNNER

As its name suggests, this bird prefers to run rather than fly. It lives in the desert scrub in the Sonoran, Mojave, and Chihuahuan Deserts. In the early morning, roadrunners bask in the sunshine to warm up after the cool night, but as the sun gets hotter, they move to bushes where it is cooler than on the ground.

LIKE A SPONGE

Male sandgrouse have specially absorbent belly feathers which soak up water like a sponge. In this way they carry water from an oasis or water hole back to their chicks, who peck at their father's feathers to take a drink. Both parents lead the chicks to solid food.

Young ostriches are dull brown and speckled to help them blend in with the colours of the desert floor

Male sandgrouse belly feathers trap water between tiny barbules (branches) coming off the barbs (main feather branches)

TOUGH BABIES

Ostrich chicks are able to run about soon after hatching, and they may travel long distances in the desert to find water and food. Chicks from several nests often band together, led by one or two adults. They grow as tall as adults (2.5 m/8 ft) after one year. Ostriches are the largest of all birds.

MAKING A HOME
A Gila woodpecker visits its nest in a giant saguaro cactus. To make the nest hole, the woodpecker hammers out the soft inner pulp of the cactus. The hole is a cool and secure place to raise young, which in the case of the Gila woodpecker hatch out blind, naked, and helpless. Another kind of woodpecker, the gilded flicker, also makes nest holes in saguaro cacti.

AT HOME
An elf owl peers out from a nest hole in a giant saguaro cactus. The hole was originally made by a woodpecker. Elf owls are one of the smallest owls in the world, reaching about 15 cm (6 in) long. They are found only in deserts in the south-west USA and northern Mexico where there are saguaro cacti.

Wing feathers are moved in such a way that the bird has perfect control over its flight

Deadly talons to catch sandgrouse and other prey

Tail feathers are used to steer in flight and are spread before landing

A hooked beak and sharp talons show this is a bird of prey

HARRIS'S HAWK
Like many birds of prey, the Harris's hawk lives in a wide range of habitats, from deserts to grassland and open woodlands in the south-west USA and South America. Unlike most birds of prey, female Harris's hawks mate with several males. Nests composed of a platform of twigs are made above ground, such as in cacti or mesquite bushes. Harris's hawks feed on a variety of animals including rabbits, lizards, flickers, and round-tailed ground squirrels.

Mammals

Small desert mammals escape the extreme climate of deserts by living in burrows. Temperatures within a burrow do not fluctuate as much as those on the surface. The deeper the burrow the better the insulation, so some desert mammals, such as jerboas in northern Africa, dig deeper burrows in summer to escape the heat. During cold desert nights, and in the winter, a burrow is warmer than the surface air. Burrows are also used to store food, such as seeds, to last when food is scarce. Many small mammals in hot deserts only come out at night or at dawn and dusk to avoid the heat of the day as well as day-active predators. If they do come out in the day or on moonlit nights, their fur colour helps them hide by blending in with their backgrounds. Some small mammals escape predators by leaping out of reach or running away.

PALLID GERBIL
A pallid gerbil can leap about 0.5 m (1.6 ft), pushing off with its strong back legs and landing on its front feet. It can also run fast. Pallid gerbils live in large burrows in the dry sandy part of north-west Egypt. They come out at night to find food, such as seeds. Gerbils have large bony projections in the skull that surround the interior of the ear. These pick up low-frequency sounds, so the gerbils can detect predators in the dark.

Long tail for balance while leaping and running

DWARF HAMSTER
This hamster is only about 8.4 cm (3.3 in) long. It comes from the desert and grassland of Mongolia, Siberia, and China, where the winters are bitterly cold. The hamster's thick fur helps to keep it warm. In the most northerly part of their range, dwarf hamsters turn white in winter so that they are camouflaged against the snow if they come out of their burrows. Like all hamsters, dwarf hamsters have big cheek pouches that they can fill with food, such as seeds, to carry back to their burrows.

SHAW'S JIRD
Jirds are related to gerbils and together they are the largest group of small mammals living in the dry regions of Africa and Asia. This large jird, with a body up to 20 cm (8 in) long, comes from Morocco, Algeria, Tunisia, and Egypt.

Tail used to help the jird balance on its hind legs

HOPPING ALONG
Kangaroos have strong back legs so they can hop along at great speed. Some small desert mammals, such as kangaroo rats from North America and jerboas (p. 37) from Africa and Asia, are like miniature kangaroos because they hop along on their back legs. For small mammals, hopping along helps them to make a quick getaway, and may also confuse the predator.

Red kangaroos live in the Australian deserts

CHINESE HAMSTER
Sitting up on its haunches helps this curious Chinese hamster see what is going on around it. Sitting up also frees its front paws to handle food, such as seeds. Chinese hamsters have longer tails than most hamsters. These hamsters are found along desert fringes and grasslands in Siberia, Mongolia, and Korea, as well as in China.

SPINY MICE
Spiny mice have stiff spine-like hairs mixed with their fur. The stiff hairs make them a little less edible, and they can erect these hairs to make themselves look larger. But their ability to shed their tails may be a greater defence: a predator grabbing a spiny mouse by its tail will be left with the tail in its mouth while the mouse gets away. Spiny mice are active in the early mornings and late evenings as well as at night. They live in rocky areas.

Spiny mice living amongst dark rocks are often a darker colour, which makes them harder to see

Egyptian spiny mouse

Rodents have continually growing front teeth

TAKING A SNOOZE
A desert kangaroo rat sleeps in its burrow in the Mojave desert of California, USA. Kangaroo rats are solitary except in the breeding season. They seal their burrows during the day so that the moisture in the air they breathe out is trapped in the burrow. This keeps the burrow humid, so less moisture is lost from the body by evaporation from the nose and mouth.

Arabian spiny mouse

KANGAROO RAT
Kangaroo rats come out of their burrows at night, hopping along on their long back legs. They move from bush to bush searching for seeds. Even on their dry diet, kangaroo rats get by without needing to drink water. They conserve moisture by producing only a small amount of urine and dry droppings. Like all rodents, they do not sweat. In an emergency, they can cool down by licking the fur on their necks.

Big ears to pick up sounds of approaching predators

Eyes positioned to give wide field of view

Strong back legs for jumping

Larger mammals

Many of the larger desert mammals, such as desert hedgehogs and foxes, spend the heat of the day in burrows, coming out at night to search for food. Even the dorcas gazelle is known to take refuge in other animals' burrows during exceptionally hot weather. Members of the cat family living in deserts often hunt at night, sheltering in rocky lairs or in any available shade during the day. Whatever the weather, meerkats are active during the day but dive into their burrows when predators approach.

Lions disappeared from the Sahara due to hunting (p. 43) and increasing dryness

(p. 43)

BIG CATS

Lions are still found in the deserts of southern Africa, where they can survive the dry season on moisture from the blood of their prey. In the past lions were more widespread, even living in the Sahara. Cheetahs still live in the Sahara but they are exceptionally rare. Cheetahs in the Kalahari often hunt during the cool of the night, instead of during the day.

SPINY ANTEATER

This strange egg-laying mammal is also known as a short-beaked echidna. Only three mammals, both species of echidna and the duck-billed platypus, lay eggs; all other mammals give birth to live young. The short-beaked echidna is found in a wide range of habitats in Australia, including the central deserts and Tasmania, as well as in New Guinea. It has a long sticky tongue for slurping up termites and ants.

DORCAS GAZELLE

These gazelles live in herds of up to 50 animals where there is plenty of grazing. They are found from northern Africa through the Middle East to Pakistan and India. Breeding males have small harems of up to seven females. When a female is ready to give birth she leaves the herd to find a secluded place. Gazelles often give birth to twins, which are vulnerable to being eaten by eagles, caracals, and hyenas.

WILD ASS

This wild ass, called a kulan, lives in the deserts of Turkmenistan (the Kara Kum and the Kyzyl Kum), in central Asia. In winter the kulan grows a rich thick coat to keep out the cold. A close relative of the kulan, called a khur, lives in the hot Thar desert of India. Herds of asses are also found in some parts of the Sahara, but these may be domesticated asses which have escaped back to the wild.

Large ears help to detect prey and to lose excess heat

Distinctive ear tufts like those of a lynx

SAND FOX

Ruppell's foxes live in in dens in sandy and rocky deserts in northern Africa and the Arabian Peninsula. They can be active during the day but often come out at night to hunt small animals. Their feet have furry soles to help them walk on sand.

CARACAL

This cat lives in a wide range of habitats including the deserts of Africa and Asia. Caracals are well known for their ability to catch birds, and can even leap into the air to swat a bird in flight. They also hunt reptiles, small mammals, and mammals as large as gazelles. Caracals sleep in caves, rocky crevices, and abandoned burrows.

Large ears radiate
heat to keep the
animal cool

Good sense
of smell to
find food

DESERT HEDGEHOG
This hedgehog comes
from the dry regions of
northern Africa, the Arabian Peninsula, and Iraq.
When threatened it rolls up to expose the spines of
its coat while protecting its soft underparts. Desert
hedgehogs dig burrows which they live in during
the day by themselves. In the breeding season, the
female looks after the young in the burrow,
suckling them for two months. Adult
hedgehogs eat birds, eggs,
scorpions, and other
small animals.

JACKALS
Black-backed jackals live in the grasslands and deserts of eastern and southern
Africa. In the Kalahari Desert they feed on a wide range of food including small
animals, birds, berries, and wild melons, which are an important source of water
in times of drought. Jackals are good at sneaking bits of meat from kills made by
other animals including brown hyenas and even lions.

RARE HORSE
Przewalski horses
once roamed the
dry lands of
Mongolia. Since
the 1960s they have
been extinct in the
wild. Fortunately,
there are still herds
in captivity which
are being bred for
re-introduction
to the wild.

MEERKAT
Meerkats live in groups in the Kalahari and
Namib deserts, and in dry open country in
other parts of southern Africa. They all work
together: as a meerkat with its head down
looking for food in the wide open desert is an
easy target for a bird of prey, one member
of each group scans the horizon from
up a bush or tree. If a predator
is spotted, the guard barks
in alarm and the group
races to the safety of a
burrow. Meerkats
also have nannies
in the group,
which take turns
to look after the
babies while the
mother is out
feeding with the
rest of the group.

Adapting to desert life

THE DESERT IS A HARSH place in which to live, yet a variety of different kinds of animals thrive there. Their bodies and behaviour are adapted to allow them to cope with extreme temperatures, lack of water, and scarcity of food. The same adaptations can be found in different animals; for example, both fennec foxes and desert hedgehogs (p. 35) have big ears to help get rid of excess heat. Some animals with different origins, such as the marsupial mole from Australia and the golden mole from Africa, look similar because they both burrow in sand, but they are unrelated. Humans too, can live in deserts as they are able to modify their surroundings to a much greater extent than animals.

UNDER WRAPS
People in their natural state are not well suited to the desert. But they can build dwellings (pp. 44–45) and wear clothes to protect themselves against the extreme heat and cold of the desert. They also have many ways to get food and drink (pp. 46–47).

CACTUS
Plants also have to adaptat to live in the desert (pp. 18–21). Cacti are succulents. To reduce the loss of water from evaporation, cacti do not have leaves. Spines protect cacti from being eaten, and help prevent heat from reaching the plant.

SANDFISH
Not a fish but a reptile (pp. 26–29), this skink (a kind of lizard) dives head first into the sand when alarmed. The sandfish's snout is shovel-shaped, with the lower jaw slung underneath so that it can dig into the sand. It moves its body in S-shaped curves to shuffle further down; when under the sand, it holds its legs against the sides of its body. The sandfish spends the night in a burrow and comes out in the early morning and late afternoon to search for insects and other small prey. The fringe-like scales on its feet help it walk across the sand surface.

Smooth scales to help the sandfish slip through sand

WALKING ON SAND
The feet of this gecko from the Namib desert are webbed to spread its weight and to stop it sinking into the sand. The gecko lives in a burrow in the sand during the day, coming out at night to search for food, such as insects.

Big eyes with slit pupils, which open wide in the dark

SINKING INTO SAND
The sand viper from the northern African and Middle Eastern deserts avoids the hottest part of the day by burying itself in the sand. By wriggling its body it disappears, leaving only its eyes and nostrils peeping out so that it can detect its prey (such as lizards), or approaching danger. The sand viper comes out of its hiding place at night, moving along the surface of the sand by side-winding (moving sideways). It is almost identical in appearance and behaviour to the sidewinder rattlesnake of North American deserts.

Sand viper makes body into S-shape

BURROWING IN SAND
The marsupial mole from the central deserts of Australia comes to the surface to eat a gecko. The big flat claws on its front legs are for scooping away sand and the tip of its snout is covered with skin for pushing into it. The mole is blind, and has no external ear parts to give it a smooth head. Like other marsupials, the mole rears its young in a pouch. Its pouch opens towards the tail so that it does not fill with sand as the the mole burrows along.

Waves pass down the body from the tail end

As the viper sinks deeper, sand covers its back

CAMELS

The single-humped dromedary and two-humped Bactrian are well suited to desert conditions (pp. 38–39). The embryo (an early stage of development) growing inside a pregnant dromedary has two humps, one of which is lost as the baby develops.

Tail held over head

SHADY TAIL

These ground squirrels live in the deserts of southern Africa. Ground squirrels are usually out and about in the early morning and late afternoon. They use their fluffy tails like parasols to keep off the sun while they look for food, eating seeds, grass, fruit, roots, insects, eggs, and small reptiles. On cool mornings they sunbathe to warm up.

White coat helps to reflect strong sun

ARABIAN ORYX

An exceptionally hardy antelope, the oryx is superbly adapted to the desert. It is small, reaching only 1 m (3 ft) tall at the shoulder, so it can shelter under shrubby trees and needs less food to keep going. The oryx can walk long distances to find new grazing and is also able to dig up bulbs and roots by pawing at the ground. It does not need to drink, getting enough water from the dew on plants. Due to overhunting, the Arabian oryx disappeared from the wild in 1979, but an international conservation effort has successfully re-introduced the oryx to part of its former range in the Arabian Peninsula.

FENNEC FOXES

These fluffy foxes are the smallest of the fox family, only reaching 40 cm (16 in) long from the tip of the nose to the base of the tail. Their big ears act like radiators, helping them to lose heat. Fennec foxes spend the hottest part of the day in their burrows, coming out at night to hunt for small animals such as insects, lizards, and jerboas (right). Fennec foxes are found in the Sahara Desert and have also been seen in the Arabian Peninsula.

KEEPING WARM

Dwarf hamsters live in the cold deserts and grasslands of central Asia. Like all small animals, they have a large surface area compared to their volume, which means they lose or gain heat from their surroundings more readily than larger animals. They need thick fur to keep warm.

Fluffing up their fur traps a layer of air between the hairs, which helps them keep warm

Soles of the feet are hairy

Ship of the desert

Warning!
Camels on the road

CAMELS CARRY PEOPLE AND GOODS through the driest of deserts, under the burning sun and through swirling sandstorms. They are well adapted for desert conditions as they can go for days without water: they conserve moisture because their body temperature can rise many degrees before they start to sweat. They also produce concentrated urine and dry dung. Camels eat tough desert plants, and survive for long periods by using the fat stores in their humps. There are two kinds of camel: the dromedary, with one hump, and the Bactrian camel, with two humps. Both kinds have been domesticated, but only the Bactrian camel continues to live in the wild.

KEEPING THE SAND OUT
Camels have long eyelashes to keep sand out of their eyes. In a sandstorm, camels keep their eyes closed and can see well enough through their thin eyelids to keep moving. Camels can also close their nostrils to stop sand getting into their air passages.

BEASTS OF BURDEN
Camels are excellent pack animals, and when properly loaded can carry as much as 260 kg (572 lb). Before cars and trucks, camels were used to transport goods vast distances across North Africa and Asia. The camels, often 50 or more in number, were tied together in single file. These caravans, as they were called, sometimes stopped overnight in inns with large courtyards known as caravanserais.

ONE HUMP
Camels do not store water in their humps. Instead, they store fat, which is gradually used up if they do not eat enough. As the fat is depleted, the hump shrinks. Dromedaries can tolerate fluctuations in their body temperature of 6°C (11°F) and they can lose up to one third of their body fluid, a loss that would be fatal to humans. To replace it, a dromedary can drink 100 litres (about 20 gallons) of water in one go.

TAME CAMEL
The dromedary was domesticated in Arabia 4,000 years ago and was taken to North Africa, India, Pakistan, and Australia.

Long legs keep the dromedary's body high off the ground, where the air can be as much as 10°C (18°F) cooler than the air around its feet

CAMELS FOR SALE

Traders sometimes travel many miles to sell their camels, as they have to this camel market in Egypt. Some of the camels are hobbled by tying one leg up; this is to stop them moving away from their owners and to stop bull camels fighting. The price of a camel depends on its breed and condition. Some camels are used for their milk and meat, some are kept as pack animals, while others are bred for riding and racing. Camel hair and skins are also used, and even camel dung is collected for fuel.

GETTING UP

A camel rests on the ground with its legs tucked under its body. It has callosities (thick patches of hard skin) on its legs and chest where the pressure is greatest. To get up, a camel first gets into a kneeling position. Then it pushes up its strong back legs before finally straightening its front legs. Riders mount a camel when it is sitting down and have to hold on tight as the camel rises, see-sawing forwards and backwards. To sit again, the camel kneels down on its front legs before lowering its back legs to the ground.

Fur in camels' ears prevents sand getting in

Like the dromedary, the Bactrian camel's two humps are stores of fat, but unlike the dromedary's hump, they flop over when the fat is depleted

RIDING ALONG

Riding camels can cover over 160 km (100 miles) in a day. Racing camels can reach average speeds of 33 km/h (20 mph) during 10-km (6-mile) races.

FLAT FEET

Dromedaries living in sandy deserts (pp. 12–13) have broad flat foot pads which help them to walk on soft sand without sinking in. Mountain dromedaries have narrower foot pads to help them walk over stony ground. Camels do not have hooves; instead their two toes end in claws. The tough soles of their feet can withstand the heat of the sand.

TWO HUMPS

Bactrian camels have two humps, and thick fur to keep them warm during the bitter cold central Asian winters. They moult (shed their thick fur) in the spring. Domesticated Bactrian camels are found in central Asia; fewer than a thousand wild Bactrian camels still survive in the Gobi Desert.

Bactrian camels have long shaggy fur which covers the upper surface of the foot

Camel regalia

THE VAST MAJORITY of the world's camels are domesticated dromedaries. Some people think of them as obnoxious, smelly beasts, but desert nomads have a high regard for their camels, and dress them in magnificent finery. Almost every part of the camel may be dressed, with pieces that are embroidered and decorated with shells, beads, mirrors, and tassels. This highly decorative regalia is brought out for special occasions such as weddings and religious festivals. Because the camel's finery is so beautiful, some of it is also used to decorate people's homes. Among most desert peoples, women generally do the weaving and embroidery, and men make the saddles and harnesses.

Eye hole

Ear hole

Net hangs down the camel's neck

Eye hole

Ear hole

FANCY HEAD GEAR
Camel headdresses are made using a variety of fabrics: the one above, from Iran, is made of sheep's wool; the finely embroidered headdress (left) with beaded tassels is made of silk and comes from Uzbekistan. They are fixed by a chain or tie under the camel's chin.

CAMEL NECKLACES
Necklaces decorate a camel's neck and shoulders. The one below comes from the Sind province in Pakistan. It is made of heavy cotton decorated with shells which are a symbol of wealth. In recent years, white glass or plastic buttons have replaced shells.

Loop to hang round the saddle's pommel

Woollen necklace made by Baluchi nomads

POM-POMS AND TASSELS
Extra pom-poms and tassels are hung from the camel's head and neck. The ones shown above are made from wool by Baluchi nomads who live around the borders of Iran.

The pom-poms are made by children

CHEST BAND
This chest band comes from Rajasthan in India, where camels are used by peoples in the Thar desert. When not on a camel, this beautiful hand-crafted piece would be draped over the doors of homes for decoration. The band at the top is cotton embroidered with silk. The long tassels are made of wool.

SADDLE
The beautifully worked wood and leather of this saddle show that it belonged to a wealthy Tuareg; it dates from the beginning of this century. The long straps are fixed under the camel's belly to keep the saddle in place.

The back of the saddle gives the rider some support on long journeys

DRAPES
Many different-sized drapes can be hung from the camel's shoulders. They are also sometimes hung inside the tent. The skill and precious materials that have gone into their making show that they were for special occasions or for rich families.

The white beads and complicated knots, called Turk's head knots, are characteristic of work from Uzbekistan

Wooden pommels project through the saddle cover

The black tassels are made of goat's hair, and the coloured parts are made of sheep's wool

BUM BAG
A crupper is for decorating a camel's hindquarters. This one is embroidered in a style typical of the Sind. In the centre of each yellow daisy is a mirror that sparkles in the sunlight as the camel walks along. The background is filled in with buttons stitched down with threads of different colours.

The cotton knee band comes from the Sind

READY TO GO
Outfits such as this one made by the Bedouin are often passed from generation to generation. The harness on the head can be fitted with reins. The saddle is a simple wooden frame which rests on a canvas saddle blanket to protect the camel. Sheepskin makes a comfortable seat for the rider. Saddle bags fringed with tassels hang down each flank of the camel; they can be used for transporting goods or personal possessions. The rider sits with the left leg hooked around the front pommel, with the right leg over the left ankle.

KNEE COVERS
A fun addition to a set of regalia, knee covers are not very common. The woollen ones above must have belonged to a sumptuous set as they are very finely woven. They were made by Baluchi nomads.

Domesticated animals

PEOPLE HAVE DOMESTICATED animals to use them for their own purposes for thousands of years. Special breeds cope with desert conditions, but livestock is still wiped out in severe drought. Even camels cannot survive the summer months without people to lead them to water and fresh grazing. Although horses are less suited to the desert, the swift-footed Arab horse is much valued. Dogs are used for their hunting skills. Sheep, goats, and cattle give milk and meat. But the fringes of many deserts have suffered overgrazing by livestock, especially where new bore wells have encouraged people to keep more animals.

A rattle made from hooves from the south-west USA

The horse's headpiece matches the royal saddle

Saddle sits on a matching saddle cloth

OSTRICH
Since ancient times ostrich feathers have been a popular form of adornment. Ostrich egg shells are also used to make jewellery (p. 60). In southern Africa ostriches are farmed for their feathers, and the skin is turned into tough leather for shoes.

Arabs carry their tails high

SADDLE FOR A KING
This fabulous horse's saddle is the livery (pp. 40–41) of the Arab horses of the kings of Morocco. It is embroidered with a mass of gold thread. The kings use this saddle on state occasions. Such finery is also presented to other heads of state.

Slender legs

SHEEP FROM THE GOATS
Both sheep and goats are kept on the fringes of deserts where there are wells for water. Goats browse on tough vegetation, and they are more tolerant of dry conditions: some breeds only need water every two days. Sheep, however, need to be watered every day. Both sheep and goats provide their owners with milk, meat, and wool. Keeping too many animals destroys desert vegetation because plants are trampled and eaten down to the ground.

ARAB HORSE
Horses were highly valued by the Bedouin for their speed and manoeuvrability in battle, and they are still much admired today. The Arab horse is the oldest breed of horse. It originated in the Arabian Peninsula over 4,500 years ago. Often dubbed the desert horse, the Arab horse has great stamina and powers of endurance. From the 7th century onwards, the Arab horse was taken to north Africa and to what is now Spain and Portugal as land was conquered for the Islamic faith.

STRANGE BEAST

Bactrian camels were domesticated about 4,500 years ago, mainly for use as beasts of burden. When people ride a Bactrian camel, they sit between the two humps.

LAST LIONS

Hunting lions from horseback required good riding skills and well-trained horses, as this 19th-century painting of an Algerian lion hunt shows. The saddle and stirrups helped give the rider a more secure seat. Lions were still common in some parts of the Sahara in the 1850s, but the last one was shot in 1932.

ZEBU

Zebu cattle are more tolerant of heat than other breeds; their fat is concentrated in a hump over the shoulders instead of in an even layer over the body. This works in the same way as a camel's hump, helping heat to escape from the rest of the body more easily. The same principle applies to fat-tailed sheep, which store fat in their tails.

"Dished" face characteristic of the Arab horse: large, bright eyes, flared nostrils and a tapering muzzle

GUANACO

The guanaco has the characteristic long, curved neck of members of the camel family. It lives wild in the Patagonian desert of South America. Llamas and alpacas are also members of the camel family and are considered by some to be the descendants of the guanaco. Llamas are kept for use as pack animals, and alpacas are kept for their wool.

SALUKIS

The Bedouin use these dogs to hunt hares and gazelles, and also when hunting with falcons. With their long legs and back, salukis are superb runners, reaching 64 km/h (40 mph). Females are preferred as hunting dogs because they can run for longer and cope with the heat better. Salukis are one of the most ancient breeds of dog: they originally came from the Arabian Peninsula thousands of years ago.

Somewhere to live

SAN HUT
Traditionally, the San (also called Bushmen) of the Kalahari Desert made shelters using branches thatched with dry grasses. Some only built these shelters in the wet season to keep the rain off. In the dry season simple wind breaks would provide shelter; warmth at night came from an open fire.

YURTS
Mongolian nomads live in felt tents called yurts. The felt is made of sheep's wool. Sheets of felt are spread over a wooden frame leaving a hole in the top for smoke from a fire to escape.

DESERT PEOPLES NEED SHELTER to protect them from the harsh climate. In some desert regions, people live in permanent homes such as the mud houses of some Native Americans of the south-west USA. Nomads, however, need portable homes which they can dismantle and take with them as they move their livestock from place to place. Whether portable or permanent, all desert homes need to be well insulated for protection against the extreme heat and cold. Airy tents of densely woven goat's hair and thick-walled homes are both suitable for desert climates. Desert dwellings also need to be waterproof, for any rain is often torrential.

BEDOUINS AT HOME
Among the Bedouin people of the Middle East and the Sahara, it is the men who receive guests in one side of the tent. The women's quarters are shielded by a woven curtain. The nomadic Bedouin have few possessions to weigh them down as they journey from place to place. Swords, guns, and coffee-making equipment, as seen in this tent, are among their prized possessions (p. 47, pp. 50–51).

BIG DISH
This Bedouin dish is large enough to hold a whole cooked sheep. Slaughtering a sheep or goat only happens on a special occasion, such as a religious festival or a visit by an important person. The men sit on the ground, and all eat from the same dish with the fingers of their right hands. Women and children eat their meal in their own quarters.

Inside the tent there is little furniture apart from floor covers and cushions

It is dark and therefore cool inside the tent

The tent is made of long strips of goat's hair often woven by the women who live in the tent

The sides and back can be lifted up to let a cooling breeze flow through the tent

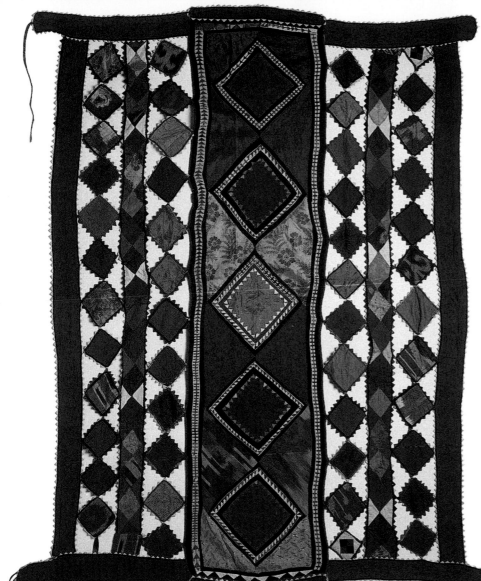

DOOR SCREEN
This 1930s patchwork camel saddle cover from Uzbekistan was also used as a doorway screen to give a bit of privacy and shade. It is made of silks and cottons, and is embroidered with cross stitch.

Native American pueblo

These underground homes in Matmata (Tunisia) have been in use for more than 2,000 years

STAYING PUT
Not all desert people are nomads. The Native Americans of the south-west USA built pueblos (villages) out of mud and wood as well as stone. The people of Matmata, Tunisia, live in cool, cave-like homes dug into the desert ground. Desert housing needs to be well insulated to keep out the heat during the day and to stop rooms becoming too cold at night. Houses are built with thick walls and small windows for insulation. Living underground provides even better insulation against both heat and cold.

BEDOUIN TENT
The tent is made of goat's hair cloth which keeps the sun off and the worst of the water off during the rare rains. The side walls are fixed to the roof and can be tied down to keep out the wind, sand, or sometimes the cold night air. After a man gets married, the size of his tent increases. A wealthy man with a big family may have several extra sections.

MOBILE HOMES
Like nomads, snails carry their homes with them.

If it rains, the fibres absorb water and expand to make the tent waterproof

The tent is supported by poles and tied to the ground with guy ropes. Women usually put the tent up

The women's quarters include their living area as well as places to sleep and cook

Modern Bedouins use lightweight plastics instead of the old wood and metal

Food and drink

SOME DESERT PEOPLES, such as the Aboriginals from central Australia and the San from the Kalahari, once survived entirely by hunting game and gathering food from the wild. Because they travelled from place to place on foot, they carried only a few hunting tools and containers for food. Nomads who have camels, such as the Bedouin from Arabia and northern Africa, can carry more possessions. Domesticated livestock also provide milk and meat. But hunting game means precious livestock need not be slaughtered. While the lifestyles of many desert peoples have changed, some old traditions continue today.

MAKING BUTTER
This Bedouin woman swings a goatskin full of yoghurt back and forth to turn it into butter. The yoghurt is made from sheep's or goat's milk which is boiled and then put in a goatskin with yoghurt from a previous batch. This introduces the right bacteria to turn the milk into yoghurt. After about an hour and a half of shaking, the yoghurt turns into butter which is then stored in a goatskin.

Boomerangs are hurled to fell game

Hook boomerang, also used as a hand-club

The spear-thrower has a hook at one end which fits into a groove or the hollow end of the spear

HUNTING DOWN UNDER
The Aboriginal peoples from the central Australian deserts hunt using a variety of simple and versatile weapons. A spear-thrower extends the length of the thrust so the spear can be thrown further. Attaching a stone knife to the wad of gum or beeswax at one end of the thrower turns it into a scraper to remove flesh from the skin of an animal carcass, or a knife to cut sinews. To light a fire, the hard edge of the thrower is rubbed rapidly against a soft stick to make sparks and ignite a tinder of dry grasses. The spear-thrower is also used as a dish.

SAN BOWS AND ARROWS
Today, only a few San hunt game with bows and arrows (p. 49). The men are the hunters, tracking down an animal, such as an antelope, and then shooting it. Quill arrows are not strong enough to kill an animal, so they are dipped in poison. The hunters follow the animal until it dies from the poison. Meat is supplemented with roots, bulbs, fruit and nuts gathered by women and children.

Hunting bags are made from an animal's skin; they are used to carry arrows and game

Cord made from plant fibre and animal hide

A bowstring is made of wood strung with sinews from an antelope's back

Poison for the arrow tips comes from a kind of beetle grub, which is squeezed and rubbed on

Metal arrowheads are bound on with sinew and gum

GAZELLE TRAP
A nasty surprise awaits a gazelle that treads on this trap used by the Tuareg people of the Sahara. The sharp stakes dig into the flesh of the leg while the noose tightens around the struggling victim. The trap is secured into the ground by the wooden stake. In the past, gazelles were often hunted for food; now they are protected, but probably still hunted illegally.

WATER BAG

A goatskin bag is traditionally used by the Bedouin to carry water. In the old days, the Bedouin relied on drawing water from wells in the desert. They planned their routes through the desert by knowing how far their water supply would last between wells. Today, Bedouin often drive into the desert with water-tankers to provide water for their livestock and their own needs.

The long woollen tie secures the neck of the bag so not a drop of precious water is spilled

TUAREG COOKING UTENSILS

Nomadic Tuaregs buy grain, such as millet, by trading rock salt which they carry through the desert on camel caravans (p. 38), selling surplus milk-products or earning money from tourism and other jobs. After threshing the grain, it is tossed in a winnowing basket to separate the edible seeds from the chaff (light husks). Millet is pounded and then cooked in pots to make a porridge eaten with a wooden spoon.

Winnowing basket

Cooking pot

Wooden spoon

This calabash has been repaired with strong stitches of grass and leather

This old bowl is well-worn and has metal patches underneath to hold it together

BREAD BOWL

Bedouin women use this wooden bowl to knead dough for bread. Pieces of dough are rotated between the hands to make large flat shapes which are cooked on a metal tray over an open fire. The dough does not contain yeast so the resulting bread is unleaven.

BREAKABLE BOWLS

Fine pottery bowls, such as this made by Zunis, are not practical for nomads. The Zunis live in pueblos (p. 45) so can keep such fragile items. This finely decorated 19th-century bowl was used to hold food. The calabash is made from a gourd (the hard fruit of a vine). Calabashes like this are treasured by the Fulani, the semi-nomadic people from the fringes of the Sahara (p. 48).

MAKING COFFEE

A visitor to a Bedouin tent is treated to coffee, prepared by the master of the tent. Once the visitors have drunk the coffee, they are under the protection of their host. To make the coffee, beans are roasted over the fire and cooled in a wooden dish. After being pounded in a mortar with a pestle, the coffee is added to boiling water with cardamom. The pounding is done to a particular rhythm, which announces to others that there are guests. The coffee is drunk from small cups, and polite guests have three cupfuls, after which they shake their cup and hand it back to their host.

Mortar and pestle

Cooling dish

The beans are roasted in this pan and turned over with the spoon

The coffee is boiled in the large pot and served from the small pot, which has cardamom added to it

The coffee is strained with a twig in the spout

This silk coffee bag must have belonged to a well-to-do Bedouin

The large bag is used to hold coffee beans and the small bag, cardamom seeds; both are made of leather, and are hung up in the tent on a tent post.

Men's kit

Weapons are not only for fighting: they are status symbols, showing a man's wealth and his position. Some desert nomads, such as the Tuareg and the Bedouin, were well known for their fighting spirit, and a man carried his weapons all the time. Now the more decorative weapons are worn only on ceremonial occasions. Other men of the desert wear different decorative items, and even paint their bodies.

This strap is slung over one shoulder, so that the sword hangs at the back

TREASURED SWORDS

The Bedouin often presented swords with elaborate inscriptions as gifts to visiting dignitaries. The Tuareg sword above would have had the handle, scabbard, and even the blade renewed as it was passed down through the generations. The blade of the sword is double-edged, making it a fearsome weapon.

This Bedouin sword has a blade that is three generations old, but the scabbard is new

Beaded cord to tie cow tail round left upper arm

GOOD LUCK

Among cattle herders in Africa, tails from hoofed animals are sometimes considered to have magical properties. Tails can also be used to whisk away flies in the same way a cow uses its tail. This cow's tail is a good-luck charm worn on the upper arm by African tribal people from Sudan.

BEDOUIN DAGGERS

Daggers were once used in skirmishes and fights, but now they are used to slaughter livestock and on ceremonial occasions. Bedouin men wear them tucked into their belts. The sheaths of these daggers are made of wood covered with silver. Dagger blades are made of steel, while the handles are made of bone, wood, ivory, horn, or plastic, and can, like these, be covered with silver.

HANDY POUCH

Tuareg men wear pouches like this round their necks to carry money and personal possessions as their robes have no pockets. This highly decorated pouch is made of embossed leather; the central green square is embroidered.

FANCY SILVER

The sheath and hilt of this 19th-century Bedouin dagger is decorated with niello. It is made by melting a special powder into dents made in the surface of the silver.

DAGGERS DRAWN

Tuareg daggers come in different sizes and designs. The men wear these daggers around their waists. Tuareg blacksmiths and craftworkers traditionally travel from one group of Tuaregs to another, making daggers, swords, and jewellery (pp. 56–57), and bringing the latest news. The men do the metalwork, and the women do most of the decorative leatherwork.

Pair of loops to attach the dagger to the belt

This leather has been stained green to look like verdigris, the crust that forms on metals such as copper, brass, and bronze when they are exposed to the air

The scabbards are made of leather decorated with silver and brass

Tuareg designs are geometric since Moslem religion does not allow artists to draw birds, animals, or people

Tuaregs are known for their high-quality leatherwork

This dagger is 38 cm (15 in) from hilt to tip

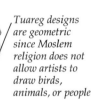

Patterns for an open ceremony do not include secret or totemic designs

BODY DECORATION

Aboriginal peoples from Australia use paint to decorate their bodies for ceremonial dances. This man is of the Arrernte people (known in the past as the Aranda), who live in the Simpson Desert.

CAMEL BACK

A fully armed Tuareg riding his camel must have been a formidable sight. Nowadays, most weapons are kept for ceremonial occasions but Tuaregs still ride camels and carry swords.

SHAVING KIT

This knife was used by Aboriginal peoples for shaving. The blade is made by carefully chipping flakes of glass off bottles. It is stuck into the wooden handle with plant resin.

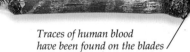

Traces of human blood have been found on the blades

This style of long rifle was made throughout the Ottoman Empire in the 18th century

FIREARMS

Firearms such as long rifles were used by the Bedouin in the 18th century. The rifle replaced the spear and made hunting game for food much easier. But game animals, such as oryx (p. 37), were over-hunted when people from towns pursued them in motor vehicles. Pistols were used by Bedouin for protection and combat in the 19th and 20th centuries. Ammunition for firearms was carried in belts or bandoliers strung boldly across the chest.

Revolving cylinder for cartridges

Women's costume

TRADITIONAL WOMEN'S COSTUMES, such as these from Jordan, are well suited to the harsh desert climate. Head coverings, long flowing robes, and layers of material provide insulation from the extreme desert temperatures and protection from the hot sun. Middle Eastern costumes in particular are modest, concealing the shape of the body and covering the arms, legs, and head. In some countries a veil, head cloth, and cloak may also be worn over the clothes when outside the home. More elaborate costumes are a sign of wealth and are only worn for special occasions. Jewellery is also worn as a sign of wealth and for its beauty; some pieces are amulets, worn to ward off evil or injury.

The bands of colour are satin stitch and buttonhole stitch

Cucumber amulet

These coins were popular for their high silver content. They were even melted down to make jewellery

BACK AND SIDES
The back and side views of the Jordanian costume show the elaborate headdress. A simple black scarf covers the woman's head and neck. The silver coins that decorate her forehead are Russian and Ottoman; the coins on the strip hanging down the back are known as Maria Theresa dollars. They were originally from the Austrian Hapsburg Empire, but were still minted long after it fell.

ZUNI BELT
This colourful woollen sash from the early 1900s was worn wrapped several times round the waist as part of Zuni women's everyday dress. The Zunis are Native North Americans who live in New Mexico and Arizona in the United States.

BASIC BLACK
Traditionally, desert dresses were made of natural fabrics, particularly cotton, like this one from the 1950s. Now they are made of synthetic fabrics as well, although these are not as cool as the cotton ones. The long amulet is called a cucumber amulet, and it contains a piece of paper with writings from the Koran (the Islamic holy book). It is decorated with crescents, the symbol of Islam. The woman is carrying a Bedouin water jug.

The headband made of silver coins is given on marriage as part of the dowry (p. 54)

The coral is from the Red Sea or the Mediterranean Sea

A matching cloak is held over one shoulder; it can also be used as a head cover

Instead of being printed on, the pattern in the fabric is created by dying the threads before the fabric is woven

Straw baskets are now more often made of nylon, since modern harvesting methods destroy the straw

COVER YOUR HEAD

Hats are useful for protecting the head from the desert glare. This hat is skillfully embroidered with a complex design from Uzbekistan. The bottom edge is rimmed with one half of a zip. This is a child's hat.

This dress is made of sateen, which is cotton woven to look like shiny satin

SUMPTUOUS SATEEN

Plenty of material was used to make this beautiful Jordanian costume from the 1930s. Using lots of fabric in this way is a sign of wealth. The woollen belt holds the extra length of the dress up so that the hem clears the ground. The right sleeve of the dress is much longer than the left, so it is rolled and pinned to the shoulder. This was simply a fashion statement of the time. The necklace is made of precious coral and silver, and the cylindrical amulet case contains writing from the Koran.

The wooden stick is for applying the kohl to the inner rim of the eyelids

Blue beads ward off the evil eye

MAKE-UP BAG

This padded silk bag was made by a Bedouin woman. It contains a small glass bottle of black eye make-up called kohl, which is made of a mineral ground to a fine powder. Kohl makes the eyes look bigger, and is popular with many Moslems and Indian women. It is also believed to protect the eyes from disease and to improve the sight. Kohl is often used on babies and children too.

Desert brides

WEDDINGS THE WORLD OVER are a time for celebrations, and great attention is paid to the bride's dress. In Jordan, the bride wears several different wedding dresses. They are then kept to be worn for special occasions thereafter. Both nomad and village brides receive silver or gold jewellery on their marriage, which becomes their personal property. They also receive gifts of money and other traditional gifts of food, such as sugar or rice. The groom and his family go to collect the bride from her family's house in a caravan of cars, with the men shooting off rifles and the women singing on the way. The wedding celebrations last for three days, sometimes longer, with the men in one tent and the women in another. Most weddings happen on a Thursday or a Friday, which is the Moslem holy day.

CAMEL BAG
This beautifully embroidered dowry bag from India would be draped over a camel carrying the bride. The complex design on the strap was drawn by men and then embroidered by women using threads coloured with vegetable dyes.

Mirrors decorate the pocket of the bag

Pockets for the dowry

The pattern is hammered on

The black design was created in niello

A bracelet made in Egypt

ALL THAT GLITTERS
A Bedouin woman is given jewellery when she gets married, and it is bought for her by the bridegroom's family or her father. A married woman's jewellery is her own property and it gives her some security for the future. She can later buy more when times are good. Early this century niello (p. 50) became popular because it can be done only on metal with a high silver content. So the purchaser knows that the silver he or she is buying is high grade. Today gold is more popular than the heavy traditional silver pieces.

The desert veil is very heavy, so it is only worn outside the home

One of a pair of silver head decorations from the Sinai desert, worn over the ears

The headdress is a separate square of cloth, embroidered to match the dress

DESERT VEIL
The designs on this 1940s bridal dress are entirely embroidered, so a great deal of care and time went into its making. The hand-woven belt is decorated with cowrie shells for luck. The band of coins over the face is known as the desert veil, and it is hooked onto the headdress with strings of beads and chains on each side. The outfit is from the Sinai (in Egypt) and also from southern Palestine.

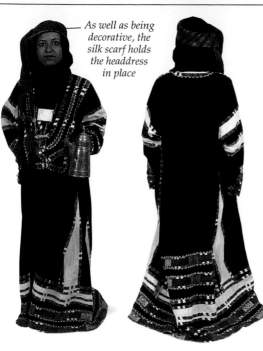

As well as being decorative, the silk scarf holds the headdress in place

AND THE BRIDE WORE BLACK

Not all cultures have special wedding colours such as the traditional white. This Jordanian bride wears a black dress from the 1950s. She also wears amulets, which are worn to bring the wearer good luck, or as a good omen. The fish is a fertility symbol and is therefore particularly appropriate for a bride. It is a popular Middle Eastern design.

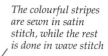

The colourful stripes are sewn in satin stitch, while the rest is done in wave stitch

A silver amulet case which can be opened to insert writings from the Koran

SILK HEADDRESS

A black silk crepe tube is fitted over the bride's head and covers her neck. The silk scarf around her head is Syrian silk shot with gold thread. She is carrying an old brass coffee pot.

A new handle has been put on to replace the old worn one

DOWRY BAG

This purse comes from Rajasthan in India, and was used by a bride to carry her dowry from her father's home to her husband's. This dowry bag is made from a beautifully embroidered square with three corners sewn together at the centre. The fourth corner is the opening flap to the purse. It is decorated with mirrors, a technique called shisha work that is common in western Asian handicrafts.

CAMEL BAG

This interwoven woollen dowry bag would be hung on the camel that carried the bride to her new home. It is from Afghanistan.

White cloth is laid over the basic fabric to offset the black and the colours

Jewellery

FOR DESERT PEOPLES, JEWELLERY is highly valued among their
few possessions. Nomads use it like a portable bank account and
sell pieces in times of hardship, such as when their livestock die
during a severe drought. The Navajo from the drylands of the
south-west USA once relied on pawning their jewellery to see
them through the winter months when no money could be
made from sheep-farming. Jewellery can be made of
everyday or valuable materials, such as silver; the latter is
often bought from traders. While some designs evolve
over the years, others stay virtually unchanged and
can be traced back over the centuries. Certain
pieces have a symbolic meaning or are
worn for good luck and to ward
off the evil eye.

*Stylized
squash
blossom*

*Turquoise of different
colours set into silver
crescent shape*

BRACELETS
Silver bracelets (above) are popular
with Tuareg women and may be
worn in pairs, one on each wrist.
They are made as a simple spike
and then curved into shape. The
design is then carved or stamped
on. The Wodaabe bracelet (right)
is made of leather decorated with
copper and brass. Wodaabe women
and girls often wear many bracelets
like these at celebrations.

TURQUOISE RINGS
The combination of silver and
turquoise is very popular with
Native American silversmiths
in the south-west USA. These
rings were made by the
Navajo. Turquoise is a mineral
found in arid regions of the
world, including New Mexico,
Arizona, and Nevada.

*These Tuareg
amulets are made
from a semi-
precious stone
called agate*

WODAABE ANKLET
The Wodaabe men pay rather
more attention to their dress and
make-up than the women (p. 48),
although this kind of anklet is worn by
both sexes. More finery is worn during
the celebrations that mark the start of
the rainy season. The highlight of these
celebrations is a charm competition
where men line up to be judged by the
most beautiful unmarried women.

TUAREG AMULETS
Some people believe wearing
amulets keeps them safe from evil
and injury, and they are usually
worn round the neck. The large
amulet is made of silver attached to
a leather loop. The round amulet is
called a tortoise amulet because
of its shape, and it is made from
old nickel-silver coins.

*Plastic
beads*

*A leather thong
is threaded through
the metal rings*

SQUASH BLOSSOM

This necklace was made by Navajo native Americans. The silver squash blossom originally came from a pomegranate fruit design worn by the Spanish who colonized the Americas in the 16th century. The crescent shape also came from the Spanish, who adopted it from the Moors, who were Moslems (p. 52). Navajos only started to work in silver in the mid-1800s, at first getting silver from melting coins and then as slugs or sheets bought from traders.

Agate necklace from the Sudan

Scented necklace from the Sind

Glass Fulani necklace

SWEET NECKLACES

Almost any material can be made into a necklace provided it can be strung around the neck. Teeth, clay, glass, silk, and stones can all be used. The necklace from the Sind province is strung with cloves as well as silk and glass beads, and the cloves still smell sweet even though the necklace is more than 50 years old. The Fulani necklace dates from early this century and was worn by young girls and men.

Aboriginal necklace, from central Australia, made of kangaroo teeth and painted gum

HAIR PIN

Decorative items can be used to adorn all parts of the body. This golden pin from Sudan would enhance any hairdo.

Ostrich shell discs

BEADS AND BAUBLES

The yellowy beads on these necklaces from the Sahel (south of the Sahara) are made from a fossil resin called copal, which is a young form of amber. It is highly prized all over North Africa. The copal in these necklaces was mined in Chad, but the necklaces themselves were strung in Niger by Tuaregs. The outer necklace also has bone, silver, glass, and ostrich shell beads.

NOT QUITE A CROSS

Some of these Tuareg crosses resemble the Ancient Egyptian ankh (symbol of life). The Tuaregs are Moslems but their silversmiths are influenced by many cultures. There are about 21 different Tuareg crosses, and men wear them to show that they belong to a particular clan. Inventive Tuareg silversmiths sometimes use recycled materials in their jewellery: the silver often comes from melted-down silver coins, and the red part from cars.

Part of the red tail light from the back of a car

Black design burnt onto bone beads

Copal is aromatic when rubbed

Spinning and weaving

ONE WAY DESERT NOMADS express themselves artistically is by weaving. Woven material can be decorative and still have a practical purpose. Wool for weaving comes from the nomads' own livestock or is bought in towns. First the wool is spun to make yarn, then it can be dyed before being woven. Heavy weaving machinery is not practical for a nomadic lifestyle, so looms tend to be light and simple. Bedouin women are highly skilled weavers, making long strips of tent cloth, tent curtains, cushion covers, saddle bags, and regalia for their camels and horses.

SPINNING A YARN
Bedouin women use cleaned sheep's wool bought in bulk, or wool sheared (by the men) from their own goats or sheep. The purpose of spinning is to line the threads up and twist them to make a strong yarn. A Bedouin woman's first job is to tease the wool apart to make it more even. Then she spins and winds the yarn on the spindle. The whole process is repeated until the spindle is full. The thread is then unwound from the spindle and looped back and forth to make a loose skein of wool.

Metal hook on top of spindle

Cross on the end of the spindle holds the wool in place

TEASING OUT
The spinner pulls out the wool and loops it around the hook on top of the spindle.

SPINNING
After quickly rolling the spindle on her thigh, she holds it up and lets it hang to spin.

WINDING
She then winds the yarn around the handle of the spindle.

Camel motif is stylized as Islam does not allow pictures of animals

CAMEL BAGS
A handy way to take goods on a camel is to pack them into bags which are attached to the saddle. Camel bags are used to carry trade goods on caravans or personal possessions when a group of nomads moves from one place to another. Abstract designs are usually woven in as the bag is made, and tassels are a popular decorative addition.

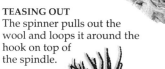

The ties are used to secure the band

CHILD'S WORK
The weaving and pattern on this camel chest band from Uzbekistan are rather uneven, which means that it was made by a girl of about ten years of age with wool left over from her mother's work. Girls are taught to weave in traditional styles by their mothers.

Synthetic dyes give much brighter colours than the more subtle natural dyes

WARP THREADS

The warp threads are stretched between the metal poles. The two sets of warp threads are held apart by a wooden blade; the shuttle is passed between warp threads to weave a weft thread.

The shuttle is simply a stick with wool wound around it

RAINBOW COLOURS

Once Bedouin women only used natural dyes to colour wool from their sheep. Now a wide range of synthetic dyes is used. Wool is dyed in skeins and then hung out to dry. The skeins have to be wound into balls before weaving. Although traditionally nomadic Bedouins used a ground loom, modern Bedouins who have settled in towns use upright looms, which are easier to use.

WEFT THREADS

After the weft thread is passed through the first set of warp threads, the second set must be pulled up; the weaver does this by hand. Now she can pass the shuttle back through to make another weft thread.

The Bedouin ground loom is a set of poles, pegs, and blocks, so it is easy to set up and transport

Peg to keep the tension of the warp threads, which is extremely important for even weaving.

USING THE BLADE

Each time the shuttle is passed through, the weaver jerks the edge of the blade back against the last weft thread to pack the thread in.

This woman has traditional Jordanian Bedouin tattoos on her face

USING THE HOOK

After a few rows, the weaver packs the weft threads down with a metal hook. The more packing or beating she does, the denser the material becomes. By tightly packing the weft threads, only the warp threads will show in the completed work.

The simplest and most easily available materials are used

Sheep's wool is softer and easier to spin and weave than goat's wool.

WEAVING A RUG

A loom can be as long as 12 m (13 yd). The widest cloth is about 3 m (3.25 yd) and needs two women to work the loom. A rug such as this one, about 4 m (4.3 yd) long, would take two or three days to make. Traditionally the Bedouin celebrated the beginning of the weaving period.

Goat's wool is reserved for tent cloth; sheep's wool is used for rugs and other furnishings

Arts and crafts

IT IS A STRUGGLE TO SURVIVE in the desert but nomads and villagers still find time to brighten their lives with beautiful things. Some have a practical use while others are made for ceremonial purposes or for pure enjoyment. Crafts are not treasured just by their creators but are often bought by tourists, and some items, such as certain Native American pottery, are highly valued by art collectors. Craft materials, such as clay and wood, can be found in the desert; other materials are a by-product of livestock. Modern materials are also used to enhance old designs.

BEAUTIFUL BEADS
Some San women and girls wear beads woven into their hair. They thread their own bracelets, anklets, necklaces, and headwear. Today they buy the beads, but they used to make them from ostrich egg shells.

SADDLE CUSHION
A cushion makes the saddle more comfortable so that the rider can endure long journeys through the desert. This leather cushion is used on the camel saddle used by the Tuareg (p. 41). The fringeless part sits behind the front pommel.

These designs are typical of Tuareg work

Single string and bow string made of horse hair

The frame is made of wood with goatskin stretched over it

BEDOUIN FIDDLE
To some ears, the Bedouin fiddle makes a rather mournful sound. Men play the fiddle around the camp fire for their guests, having learnt how to play as children. The Bedouin are well known for their hospitality and, as part of their way of life, will give food and shelter to strangers in the desert.

ROCK ART
The inscriptions on this rock from the desert in Jordan date back at least 2,500 years. It shows a herd of healthy camels (with fat humps) and their youngsters. Rock art is found in many deserts and gives clues as to what these places were like in the past and who lived there (pp. 6–7).

This photograph dates from the turn of the century

SILVER AND GLASS
Tuareg silversmiths used to make their wares for the Tuareg nobles, but many now stay in towns where they work for the tourist trade. They make Tuareg crosses using a process called the lost wax method: the form is carved in wax and a mould is built around it. The wax is then melted and poured away. Melted silver is poured into the empty mould, and when it is solid, the mould is pulled apart to reveal the cross. Finally, the surface is worked to create the patterns.

The inscription, in classical Arabic, is a verse from the Koran. It is worn to give protection to the wearer.

HOPI DOLL
Hopi Native Americans are dryland farmers from Arizona. They make dolls, called kachinas, to teach their children about their beliefs in spirits of plants, animals, ancestors, and even places. Kachina is also the name given to the spirits themselves and to masked dancers who represent the spirits at ceremonies, some of which are to bring rain. The dolls are carved from the roots of cottonwood trees and then coated in white clay before being painted.

Modern kachinas are painted with poster paints

This design represents feathers

PERFECT POTTERY
Pottery has been made by Native Americans in the south-west USA for at least 1,600 years. Pots are made for cooking, storing foods, and for ceremonies. These unusual black pots were created by the famous potter Maria Martinez from San Ildefonso in New Mexico. She invented the distinctive colour by using special clay and sand from the desert, and adding cow manure to the fire; the pots had to be fired at exactly the right temperature. She used the traditional open kilns, which are difficult to use since a gust of wind can easily ruin the whole firing.

The design is burnt and stained into the wood

MADE FOR TWO
This camel saddle frame, made for a dromedary, can hold two people. It is used by nomads trading in the Sind province in Pakistan and Afghanistan. Such a fine saddle would belong to a tribal chief. The wood is overlaid and inlaid with brass for decoration and strength.

DIDJERIDU
Although didjeridus are not traditional desert instruments they are now widely used by many Aboriginal peoples. Traditionally, they were made from branches that had been hollowed out by termites. A suitable branch was found by walking through the bush tapping on trees listening for a hollow sound.

Exploring the desert

WILFRED THESIGER
Thesiger was one of the first Europeans to explore the world's most infamous desert, the Empty Quarter (Rub al Khali) of the Arabian Peninsula. The desert gets its name from being so inhospitable; no one lives there except in the winter months, when the Bedouin visit it to graze their camels on plants that have sprung up after rain. Thesiger made several journeys on camel-back through the Empty Quarter and Oman with his Bedouin companions, covering thousands of miles between 1945 and 1950.

DESERTS ARE AWESOME PLACES, where those unaccustomed to their harshness risk dying of thirst and starvation. For centuries, explorers have been lured into the desert, seeking fame and fortune. Explorers often used established trade routes such as the Silk Road to the Far East, or helped to develop new routes, like Burke and Wills, who crossed the central deserts of Australia. Explorers often relied on local people to help them find their way: without compasses or maps, desert dwellers such as Aboriginal peoples could find their way through the desert. Desert inhabitants also had the knowledge of how to find food and water in the desert while many explorers had to go laden with supplies. Today, the deserts have all been mapped but the dangers still exist and with new ways to travel, there are still adventures to be had.

COMPASS
A compass has a needle that turns to align itself with the magnetic north and south poles. Ever since the compass was invented, probably in Europe and China in the 12th century, this instrument has helped people find their way.

ON THE WAY TO TIMBUKTU
The German explorer, Heinrich Barth, crossed the Sahara Desert in 1850, and spent several years in the fabled city. Timbuktu began as a Tuareg settlement in the 12th century, and developed into an important trading point for gold, salt, and slaves, and a centre of Islamic scholarship. The first European to reach the legendary city was the Scottish explorer, Gordon Laing, in 1826. The French explorer René Caillié also made it to Timbuktu in 1828 but few believed he had actually been there until his account of the city was confirmed by Heinrich Barth.

SAHARA BY BIKE
Modern bicycles are so tough and lightweight they can be ridden long distances across difficult terrain. For anyone exploring the desert, clothing to protect the skin from sunburn is essential. A bicycle repair kit and adequate supplies of food and water are also vital.

Head covering to prevent sunburn and overheating

Water bottle

Baggage evenly distributed over the bicycle

DEATH AT COOPER'S CREEK
The first European crossing of Australia was from south to north, starting at Melbourne. Robert Burke and William Wills led the expedition, leaving a group at Cooper's Creek on the way. The project experienced many problems, including death from starvation and exhaustion. Burke died at Cooper's Creek (above) on his return southwards in 1861. Only one of the final team survived, with the help of Aboriginals.

The wing is stretched over a frame supported by wires

G-MIJK

One person sits behind the other

The person in front grips this bar

Propeller

Engine

SAHARA BY MICROLIGHT
Christina Dodwell is a modern British explorer who likes to use unusual modes of transport on her journeys. For her 11,265-km (7,000-mile) journey across Africa via the Sahara, she chose a microlight. With her co-pilot, she flew this tiny aircraft across the astounding landscape of the Sahara. Here, they have stopped off in Mali.

MARVELLOUS MICROLIGHT
Because they fly so slowly, microlights are able to fly much closer to the ground than other light aircraft, so the passenger and pilot can see much more of what is happening beneath them. They can also travel as high as airliners, to avoid a bumpy ride through low layers of turbulent air. A microlight can land in 69 m (75 yd) on any reasonably flat piece of ground. Weighing only 150 kg (330 lb), the machine can be packed into the back of a truck.

SILK ROAD
Silk was one of the most valuable goods to be exported from China. The Chinese domesticated the silk worm thousands of years ago, getting from each cocoon a silk thread up to 900 m (3,000 ft) long. Silk was traded overland along a route called the Silk Road. This covered 7,000 km (4,300 miles) from China in the east via the mountains and deserts of Central Asia to Europe in the west. Silk and spices went west, in return for wool, gold, silver, and horses.

TRADE BEADS
These glass beads were made in the 18th century for trade with Africans, especially those living in West Africa. They could be exchanged in Africa for food, precious stones, metals, and art work.

MARCO POLO GOES EAST
In 1271 Marco Polo set off for the Far East with his father and uncle, both Venetian merchants. They followed the Silk Road through Mesopotamia (Iraq), Persia (Iran), Afghanistan, and across central Asia and the Gobi Desert to China. Marco Polo was employed by the Kublai Khan and travelled on missions throughout his great Mongol empire. The Polos eventually returned to Venice in 1295. Marco's published account of his travels gave the Europeans an astonishing account of the Far East.

Index

Acknowledgements

Dorling Kindersley would like to thank:
In Jordan, for their generous, unstinting help: K. D. Politis; Hiyam Khateeb and Sami Ajarma of the Ministry of Tourism and Antiquities; Hammad Hamdan; Tony Howard, Di Taylor; Suleiman Hamdan; Jamal As'hab; Abdellah Mohammad; Mazieb Atieeq; Mahmoud; Sabhah; Aryouf Ajaleen; Um-Magab; Widad Kamel Kawar and her daughter and friends; Imman Alqdah at the Folklore Museum, Amman; Dr Jonathan Tubb and colleagues.

For kindly providing props and help:
Moira and Margaret Broadbent; B & T World Seeds; Joliba; London Zoo; Mark O'Shea; Pitt Rivers Museum, University of Oxford; Debbie Platt; David Gainsborough Roberts; Peter Rodway; Twycross Zoo (Vera Richards, Michael Darling, John Campbell, Janet Hall,

James Bayley, Denise Cox, Alan Bates, Sonia Chapman, John Voce, John Ray); Dr David H. Thomas at the School of Biology, University of Wales at Cardiff; David Ward, Dr Jeremy Young.

For design help: Manisha Patel and Sharon Spencer; for editorial help: Helena Spiteri. Map pp. 6–7: Sallie Alane Reason. Artworks p. 13al, p. 15cl: Andrew Nash. Yurts, p. 44: Ts Davaahuu. Kachina doll, p. 61: William Lomayaktewa. Index: Ann Barrett.

Picture credits
a=above, b=below, c=centre, l=left, r=right
Ardea, London Ltd/Ian Beames: 17c; /Kenneth W. Fink: 16c; /Mike W. Gillam: 36bc; /Clem Haagner: 35ar, 37ac; /Peter Steyn: 20 bl; /Alan Weaving: 12–13b, 17br.
British Museum: 13a.
Caroline Cartwright: 18al, 19br.

Lester Cheeseman: 39al.
Bruce Coleman Ltd/Jen and Des Bartlett: 31ac; /M.P.L.Fogden: 25acl; /Jeff Foott: 6cl, 22bc, 33acl; /Carol Hughes: 6cl; /Steve Kaufman: 37ar; /Rod Williams: 35al.
Compix/E.Terry: 44al.
Philip Dowell: 38–39c.
e.t.archive: 63bc.
Mary Evans Picture Library: 7bc, 11acr, 43cr, 45ar, 49acr, 62c.
Robert Harding Picture Library/Elisabeth Weiland: 49ar.
Hutchison Library/Christina Dodwell: 63cr; /André Singer: 51cr; /Leslie Woodhead: 48ar; /J.Wright: 49br.
Image Bank/Ted Janocinski: 11ar.
Impact Photos/Ian Cook: 44–45b; /Penny Tweedie: 25br.
Mike Linley: 17ac, 18bcl, 25acr, 26bl, 27al, 29ar, 30cr, 34cr, 63b.
MacQuitty International Photographic Collection: 9bcr, 14acr, 45cr.
MountainCamera/Chris Bradley: 21bc,

51c; /John Cleare: 62br; /Matt Dickinson: 62bl.
Peter Newark's Pictures: 61ac.
N.H.P.A./A.N.T.: 12al, 16bl; /Anthony Bannister: 18acl, 19cr, 23cr, 36bcl, 60al; /Peter Johnson: 28bl, 49bl.
Christine Osborne/Middle East Pictures: 42cl.
Oxford Scientific Films/B.G.Murray Jr, Earth Scenes: 8al; /Owen Newman: 31al.
Axel Poignant Archive: 46cl.
Premaphotos Wildlife/K.G.Preston-Mafham: 16cr.
Trevor Springett: 15ar.
© Wilfred Thesiger. Reproduced by permission of Curtis Brown. Photo – Royal Geographical Society, London: 62al; Vernet's The Lion Hunt reproduced by permission of the Trustees of the Wallace Collection: 43al;
Tony Waltham: 15br, 42b;
Jerry Young: 28bcl, 28bc, 28br, 34ar, 34–35b, 35bc